Think About it...

Life Applications of the Holy Spirit

Copyright © 2021 by Brian Smith, DDS Publishing

1st Edition

This is a work of fiction. Names, characters, places and incidents are either the product of the author's imagination or are used fictionally. Any resemblance to actual persons or organizations, living or dead, is entirely coincidental.

No part of this book may be reproduced in any manner whatsoever without written permission, except in the case of brief quotations embodied in the critical articles and reviews.

Printed and bound in the USA.

Cover design, symbols, characters, names, music, artwork, interior layout, are film protected.

ISBN: 978-0-9991641-6-7

TABLE OF CONTENTS

THE RIB	6
THE POTTER'S HAND	8
THE PAINTER'S HAND	12
THE RIGHT THING	15
THE REAL MAN	18
CLEAR VISION	20
THE ROLE OF EVIL	23
THE BELIEVER	25
THE INVITATION	28
THE COOL-AID	30
THE BAKER'S MESSAGE	32
THE RELATIVES	35
YOUR THOUGHTS	37
THE TRINITY	39
RIGHTEOUS ANGER	42
BACK DOOR	43
SINGLENESS	46
THE KNEEL	48
THE NAME	51
BLENDED FAMILY	54
THE TEACHERS	57
ALL LIVES MATTER	59
PARENTAL LIES	61
THE DOG COMPARISON	65
HISTORY LESSON	68
TWO ENEMIES	71
THE INVISIBLE WORLD	73
GOD'S TIMEPIECE	75
BELIEVE IN MIRACLES	77
TRAP FOR FOOLS	78
WORRY IS USELESS	79
INTELLECTUALISM	81
THREE VS. THREE	83
ANGER IS A CHOICE	84
OUR PLANS	85
SLOW DOWN, STOP, & CARE	87
BE HUMBLE	89
HARDENED HEART	91
COLOR OF THE HEART	93
THE ORCHESTRA	95

FIVE STAR RATING	96
THE RACIST	98
THE MOUNTAIN	100
THE TRUTH	102
COVETING	105
GOD'S OPINION	107
WHO ARE YOU?	109
HATE	111
THE DEFINITION	112
LAZY SERVANT	114
DISTRACTED CHRISTIANS	117
WHY GO TO A CHURCH?	119
THE PARABLE OF THE SOWER	122
SLAVE VS. NO-SLAVE	124
YOU VS. JOB	127
THE STORY OF THREE'S	129
MAN VS. MANKIND	131
CHOOSING GOD	133
CREATING SECOND, THIRD, AND FOURTH LEVEL VICTIMS	135
PRODIGAL SONS	137
FINAL THOUGHTS	140

Life Applications of the Holy Spirit

The Rib

Have you ever wondered why God choose to use a rib bone to shape Man's companion, Woman, from? Why the rib bone? Why not a different bone? What is the purpose of the rib bone in life, and what does the rib bone represent? Maybe God chose it because it is the rib cage which surrounds and protects the Man's heart from damage or death? Couldn't God have just as easily chosen a bone from another part of him like: Man's hands perhaps to help him in his daily work, or perhaps from his leg maybe to help have an easier journey throughout his life, or, how about from his head, maybe to help give him clearer thoughts in decision making that involves his future, or perhaps from his fore-arm to perhaps help him find his way better in the dark? No, God chose none of these other bones...

God chose the rib-bone for a specific reason I believe... And if you have been blessed to have a good woman in your life for very long you will know what that exact reason is...[1]

I believe God choose to use a piece of Man's rib-bone to create his companion from because women know best how to protect, nurture, and feed a man's heart in Godly ways. The question is do all women do that for all men?

Women are born differently with an innate instinct and a sense of danger that men do not have. They also bring with them a greater need for security, and can provide service with a better smile. God chose the woman, Mary, to bear His son and share Christ's blood,

---

[1] Genesis 2:18

which no man was ever given the honor to be that close to Him on earth like his mother.

Women also understand women better than men, so maybe this can help a protect a man's heart better from some difficult challenges that he may not be aware of in a woman's world which can be a daunting task for the immature, perhaps protecting him from harm arriving in different forms or fashions.

Once again, have you ever wondered why God chose the rib-bone to fashion Man's help mate and companion from? ... Studies have shown that men who have been married for long periods of time live longer and do better than single men[2].... So, look around and see who are the happiest and longest living men in your age group. Does anyone you ever wonder why?

My parents were married for 73 years. I believe they were a great example to three generations and to our family to what I am expressing and the blessings found therein.[3]

...Think about it.

---

[2] Ecclesiastes 4:9-12
[3] Psalms 23

Life Applications of the Holy Spirit

The Potter's Hand

One of my most prized possessions is an oddly shaped coffee-mug which was given to me by one of my children after being created for an elementary school field trip. This beautiful thing was created and shaped from a hunk of amorphous clay into an exquisite shape of pottery. It had to be fired in a very hot kiln to harden the clay once shaped and then afterwards painted, and then fired again to be adorned with its colored coating which made it stick and made it beautiful…. Life is a lot like this process!

Did you know that becoming a Christian is like making a beautiful piece of pottery that the Holy Spirit will use for His purpose? Oh yes, becoming a Christian is a long and lengthy process and is allot like making a useful shape of pottery out of a useless piece of clay. The creation process is quite the opposite of an evolving process like stones or diamonds which are made perfect by nature using longer periods of time. In creation, every piece of pottery is made somewhat more quickly and it has inherent defects or flaws which can be found and uncovered if a seeker can look hard enough. but this is not a bad thing.[4]

"Believers in Christ", are internally-defective creations (sinners) who have been repurposed and taught how they were made from the ground, with elements taken from of the earth, and then made into something special and useful, just like a piece of clay pottery made with God's delight, for He said, "You are like the clay in the potter's hand, and I am the potter. This is a message from the Lord." [5]

---

[4] I Corinthians 6:11
[5] Jeremiah 18:1-9

I know of people today whose lives who are being spun out of control, twirled, and shaped with care (perhaps from the 2020 pandemic fear, the presidential election outcome, family stress, quarantine, or just life in general, etc...) into an exquisite vase made of clay, or a simple mug which later they will be able to pour themselves out into others with what the Holy Spirit will fill them in with by changing them from their un-useful amorphous stage in life, to a God-centered useful stage. This happens only with being work hardened and trusted with God's enlightenment that everything in own's life can be used for God's own glory as He will always make drinkable lemonade from His sour lemons, and there are no exceptions[6].

But, some of individuals in order to become useful souls for God's divine purpose, they need to go into the kiln to be fired more than once or twice to be made into a new creation like the exquisite pieces of pottery made from amorphous clay that we hope in prayer and faith do not crack nor break in the forming process.[7]

And I know of certain people today, who have never been even to the potter's fire,[8] still in the que, being prepared for better clay, waiting just to be selected, as they still endure in a non-useful amorphous state of clay which has no shape nor design in their lives because they have received their God-Given purpose yet.[9]

And for those few who have gone through the fire and have come out reborn and structurally changed,[10] these new vessels never choose to go back into the fire. These are highly valued[11] select people who were once lumps of clay made into useful pieces of pottery whom the Lord has shown His mercy after being tested and humbled[12] like with perhaps with the loss of a child, a divorce, severe financial crisis, health problems, disease, disability, mental

---

[6] James 1:17-19
[7] I Corinthians 10:13
[8] Matthew 22:14
[9] Psalms 57:2
[10] John 3:5
[11] Matthew 10:29-31
[12] I Peter 3:3-4

Life Applications of the Holy Spirit

disease, addiction, or the like, etc... And even after the first fire has cooled, maybe these have not been made externally beautiful yet until they go into the fire a second time to be adorned.[13]

But then also, there are certain people who disbelieve in God's firing process so much that they run and avoid it. There is something which happens to these individuals early in formation on their inside which can be quite brutal and ever-lasting thus creating a cold and hardened heart[14]. These people lack the essential character of kindness separating them from mankind, as only man can do. But this does not have to be because God is in control. These cannot see nor hear other than what they themselves spew in a world which they cannot understand.[15]

The new internal changes of being work hardened like clay into pottery and reborn and repurposed gives better and greater life structurally which makes the selected individual[16] into a new person and now useful to the Holy Spirit to do "His will"[17] with someone who can selflessly pour themselves out now into others without question or hesitation[18] ... because being a Christian is an action(s), like being a living verb, and not a living noun.

Are you perhaps going through a first, second, or third fire of God's choosing for you now in your life? Is perhaps another of God's humbling fires is quickly brewing, getting hotter, and getting ready to take you down into the kiln one more time? Has your end occurred where you have been adorned with God's holy graces and mercies so you can then pour yourself out into others selflessly with the love of the Holy Spirit and only His desire? Or are you still in the making and just need a little more time in the process?

If you do not fully understand, maybe the fire you are experiencing is a different kind of fire of mortal equalizing which

---

[13] Mark 4:16-17
[14] 2 Timothy 4:3-4
[15] John 6:44
[16] I Thessalonians 4:16-17
[17] I Peter 2:15
[18] Philippians 2:17

keeps happening over and over with no way out because you have not found God in a purpose driven life to make yourself beautiful in His own eyes yet (and not yours) …I am just saying…We are all made from the Potter's hand in one way or another…

…Think about it.

Life Applications of the Holy Spirit

The Painter's Hand

Have you ever watched Bob Ross in awe like myself as he paints his beautiful landscapes on the public television channel? He is a fantastic instructor, as well as a master painter. Bob Ross has passed on now (July 4th, 1995), but his television show still graces the airways today with his legacy of mesmerizing skills and easy-going ways. Bob constantly admitted that he was a conventional painter until he changed and moved away from his agony and learned his new ways…He also constantly said, "there are no mistakes in a painting, just a new opportunity to go with what is there, and make it better by adding another layer or two of paint". In fact, his whole technique was based on just about adding more and more layers of paint (one after the other) so that in the end… finally a beautiful picture was created. Wow, what a great thought! … with never a bad ending to any painting. We should all be so lucky!

What happens to me when I am watching Bob Ross paint, I eventually fall into full astonishment of "what could he paint next"? Then: "whatever it is… it will be beautiful"! The expectation of grandeur can become almost over whelming for anyone who is watching such a master of a teacher who cares so much as they teach their students,[19] and at the same time show a personal talent that is live and in action.

Living in faith and walking with the Holy Spirit is allot like watching the famous Bob Ross paint. The biggest difference is that Bob Ross is painting a two-dimensional painting while the Holy Spirit is painting a person's life as a legacy in 3D. Bob Ross's

---

[19] Luke 6:40, Matthew 10:24

paintings eventually will all fade away with time but the life and legacy of a person who the Holy Spirits paints never fades away.[20]

And just as in Bob Ross's words: "there are no mistakes in making a painting, just the opportunity to add more and more layers upon layers to finally make something beautiful" is the same for The Holy Spirit. They both create something for everyone to enjoy. There are no mistakes walking with the Holy Spirit, only the opportunity to become more beautiful with more layers of paint, ultimately receiving joy in the journey.[21]

So, each of us (each individual) comes into this world like a blank canvas, with nothing painted on it, but leaves eventually as some kind of picture in others' minds. (My mother used to tell me, "every person is like a blank sheet of paper without any writing on it yet, and that is where I get this analogy). No paint has been added to a person life until the person starts to think and grow. And with passing of time, the painting begins to take shape, and it continues until death. Sometimes the first colors are not happy colors that get applied, nor when the first image begins it is not a pretty one. But all this can be changed by adding more layers upon layers over the old painting. In fact, simply by just putting one's faith in Jesus Christ as a Savior, is like making the old canvas completely white again, and starting a new painting.[22] It is what is called a "do-over." How neat is that! The old picture is no longer visible, and it becomes an old thing of the past that is nowhere to be found!

---

[20] I Corinthians 13:8
[21] Galatians 5:22-23
[22] Revelation 21:5

Life Applications of the Holy Spirit

So, what does the painting of your life look like? Does it have a name? Is it good or bad? Is it something to show in an art gallery or hide in the bottom of a closet? Are you stuck in a 2D frame or a 3D world of depth? A born-again person has depth, and can be measured by his or her fruit.[23] If you do not have fruit in your life, or as commonly referred to as born again, you might want to become a 3D person.

...Think about it.

---

[23] Galatians 5:22-23

Brian Smith

The Right Thing

Most people believe that by doing "The Good" Thing[24], they must be doing "The Right" Thing[25] and then their result most certainly will be "The Best" Thing[26]… But this is certainly not true for all man's efforts in a fallen world.

History will prove that while most men get into power by promising others the "Good Things" they will do for them once given the power to do so…that when hard time come to be accountable, most everyone including elected officials do not retain the will power or stamina to do the higher calling of doing the "Right Things" on earth…only a few will ever do the right thing which will also be the righteous thing, and these will be hated for a having higher standard than the people they chose to serve? But who will choose the definition of righteousness of than Jesus?[27] It must be the Holy Spirit because men who force secular high standards on the people when it is their choice to choose their own standards makes the difference in whether they do good or evil without the proxy of an intermediary.[28]

Jesus said, "Forgive them for what they do" as his enemies nailed Him to a wooden cross and tortured Him. He lived by highest standards possible, but those around Him hated Him for it because He asked them to also follow Him in the high standards God called

---

[24] Galatians 6:9
[25] Colossians 2:7
[26] Romans 5:15
[27] Philippians 3:9
[28] Romans 14:7

Life Applications of the Holy Spirit

Him to do and for others to also do the same with the help of the Holy Spirit.[29]

So, have you forgiven your enemies lately with the help of the Holy Spirit? Say what??? Ok, then do you have enemies other than yourself? Just check the words you use and you will find out who your enemies are you need to forgive. What enmity do you hold that really holds you that causes you to feel this way?

Jesus told Peter in his moment of weakness, "Peter, get behind Me!" when Peter wanted retribution and wanted to take vengeance against his worldly enemies. But in saying this, Christ was teaching that there is no righteousness in any person when they look at themselves and see no sin. Remember when Jesus told a crowd who wanted to stone a woman for her bad actions, "Let him who is without sin can cast the first stone"; but they all walked away without doing so because no one was more righteous standing in the presence of Jesus, The Christ.

So, which person from history in the Bible are you emulating today: those who wish to cast stones while they still have sin in your own hearts?... or perhaps, like Peter, who wanted to take out his vengeance to justify his history of being a victim? Or like Jesus, who led by His example all the way to the cross, and offering salvation to all by saying, "Forgive them for what they do".

---

[29] John 14:26

The concept of "Tit-for-Tat-Vengeance or Righteous Anger" has never solved anything in this world when used by human hands or minds; and it is for this effort that makes the world a worse place to be who live in it.... And then make people want to hurt themselves when things do not go their way or they want to hurt someone else.... I am just saying...Look for someone to forgive who does not deserve forgiveness today, because the world survives on forgiveness; then you will be able to "Do the Right Thing" which may not be "The Good Thing" but it will be in the end "The Best Thing"

...Think about it.

Life Applications of the Holy Spirit

The Real Man

Question: Are there any REAL MEN out there? Or is this just a dream gone by?

What is your definition of a REAL MAN? Here is what I heard once upon a time… And I am just passing this along the best I can recall…Defining A REAL MAN is a four-step process:

Step 1[30]… "R" = "Resist Passivity"
Step 2[31]… "E" = "Expect the Best"
Step 3[32]… "A" = "Accept the things you can't change then move on"
Step 4[33]… "L" = "Lead by Example"

If you find you are too passive in life...quickly understand that by doing nothing, you have acted just as wrong as if you did the wrong thing. An elephant in the room will always come back to haunt you sooner or later. Always expect the best…No-one likes being around a negative "cup-always-half-empty" person. You serve no-one, no- cause and no- crusade by always being negative. Stop it! This is a lack of character. It only brings others down and is no way to influence people or get positive results. And, if a person cannot accept things they cannot change, that person only becomes more bitter, lonely, and hateful as they grow older. They will always see them-self as the ultimate victim; and they do not know Jesus, and

---

[30] James 4:7, 5:6
[31] Philippians 1:20
[32] Matthew 10:14
[33] I Peter 5, I Corinthians 11:1, Hebrews 13:7, I Timothy 4: 11-16, Nehemiah 5:14-19

need Him badly. Wisdom comes by discernment, and discernment leads to greater wisdom. Learn to lead from the front of the pack, and not from the back.

Only a lead sled dog or lead goose in flight, can take the rest of the pack or flock and the and any weight they are pulling in the right direction. Those pulling or in flight in the back cannot see where their future is nor what evil lies ahead. In the back is where all the surprises happen so beware, always choose to be the leader. Then after completing Step 4, and if you look around and there is no-one following you, or standing with you, pulling with you, or holding on tightly beside to you in affirmation that you are a REAL MAN…then repeat Steps 1 through 4 until you get it right.

…Think about it

Life Applications of the Holy Spirit

Clear Vision

When I was in elementary school, I was not a great student. It was not because I did not apply myself, but because I could not see very well. I inherited bad genes resulting in poor eye sight. It runs in my family, and is even worse in my siblings, with macular degeneration.

When I was about in the fourth grade my life changed for the better. My mother took me by the hand to visit an optician in McAllen, Texas at TSO on Main Street to get reading glasses. I never will forget walking out their office door and being able to see crystal clear. It was truly a startling and amazing experience! Actually, it was life changing...

I remember so vividly being able to see that all the trees actually had leaves! It was like a miracle had happened to me, and I remember I was so happy as well as in shock of what I had been missing out in life!!! Up until this point in my life everything had been a fuzzy blur...The chalk boards at the school, the car lights at night driving with the family, and all the people's faces from far away were indistinct in my own eyes. But now, I rejoice and thank God every day for the person who He helped invent glasses for clearer vision in every aspect, and in every way!

Back in that day, science had not developed light-weight poly carbonate lenses vs. heavy thick plastics just yet... Since I could barely see the "Big E" being tested using the sight chart my sight was bad. Then shortly after, my teen years were spent with wearing the dreaded "coke-bottles" as my glasses lenses, but who cares?... I could see! And so happy I could see, nothing could spoil my day, nothing! ... And you know life is allot like that. Clear vision makes all the difference about a person's attitude and gratefulness. This leads to being able to see and understand what is around you from a true sense, not a false sense. This is called discernment[34] on our earthly level, and then wisdom[35] on the spiritual level. What I thought what had happened to me was as close to a miracle I could ever envision, so from this point I believed I had received a physical state of healing. I was grateful then and still am today. In reality, our physical healing and our spiritual walk are tied closely together: evident in our actions, our words, and our prayers poured out in the form of purity so that this can be done and advocated by the will of the Holy Spirit.[36]

So, did you know that Jesus performed about 37 miracles in about 37 months? He averaged about one per month when He was traveling around, and much of the rest of the time He spent in prayer and teaching. And FYI, He did not heal everyone in His path during His ministry. I believe that He walked right past many people who wished that He would heal them, but nobody knows if this was the way it was. But what we Do Know was of the 37 recorded miracles, at least 4 of them (10%) where to give or restore people's sight. (Matthew 9:27-31, 20:29-34, Mark 8:22-26, & John 9:1-12). Why would seeing clearly be so important to Jesus? He could have just fed people with fish, or just healed lepers, but he gave people back their sight when it had been lost.

I believe He was teaching at the time and He selectively did these miracles, to show not the physical healing but that spiritual healing that comes with it according to faith. In fact, Jesus said, "According to your faith let it be done to you"[37]; and their sight was restored. So, how important is faith to you? Can you see clearly without faith? You may have great human eyesight with great vision physically, but how is your spiritual eye-sight according to your faith?

---

[34] Philippians 1:9-10, Hebrews 4:12, Romans 12:2
[35] James 1:5
[36] John 16:13-15
[37] Matthew 9:29

Life Applications of the Holy Spirit

Jesus also said, during His ministry, "Truly I tell you, if you have faith like a grain of mustard seed, you can say to this mountain, 'Move from here to there,' and it will move. Nothing will be impossible for you."[38] So, do you have a mountain or two you need moved today?... or worse by tomorrow? I would like to know if do you have enough faith measured by the size of a mustard seed? If you do there will be no mountains in your life to stand in your way, Jesus promised. But if you don't, I believe maybe you should locate some good sturdy and durable shoes because you have a very BIG mountain to climb coming up, and just maybe… many more to come, when you get finished with that one.

...Think about it.

---

[38] Matthew 17:10

Brian Smith

The Role of Evil

I guess you have heard about or read the story about Adam and Eve in the Garden of Eden …So, what are your biggest take-aways that you remember from the story? One in particular will speak to you. One will impact you. What is it? Read it at least once a year and you will learn a new perspective each time. There are so many, so let's focus on one.

Let us remember who was there in the story: Adam, Eve, God, and guess who else …the serpent. So, why do you think the story did not just say "The Devil" was there? Why did story have Satan to be in disguise? The bigger question is why in the world didn't God just get rid of him then, and just be done with him so Adam and Eve could get back to living in eternal bliss, just like they were doing before the snake (i.e., the Devil) shows up in disguise? Certainly, as the powerful creator over man and the angels, God could have destroyed the serpent right then, but He did not. If He did, we would all be living today in harmony on earth without the Devil, but this was not the will of God…Why?

So, let's now discuss the role of "Evil"[39]… The dictionary in human "man-speak" defines it as "profoundly immoral and wicked, especially when regarded as a supernatural force". In the Garden story, God tells Adam and Eve: "Do not eat or touch of one tree which I have placed in the middle of the Garden, or you will surely die (i.e., suffer forever)". But the serpent (aka The Devil in disguise) "says to both the man and the woman (and contradicts what they were told by God), "Go ahead and eat of the fruit, you shall not die…" In doing this, the action drives man and woman apart. They

---

[39] 2 Thessalonians 3:3, Ephesians 6:11

Life Applications of the Holy Spirit

both sinned. In the story, neither Adam or Eve will take any responsibility for their actions.

When I was a child, there was a comedian named "Flip Wilson". His favorite comedy laugh-line was "The Devil made me do it!" There is allot of truth to that.... I define evil as anything or anyone in disguise who is telling us what we can or can-not do speaking in place of what God has already told us what we can or can-not do. My definition of "Evil" is: the sinister result of packaging lies within the smile of deceit. My mother would say that evil is best discussed as a "wolf in sheep's clothing" from telling me bed time stories. So, why doesn't anyone read the story Little Red Riding Hood to their children anymore? Oh, the world is misled so much these days by the evil of deceit.[40] It is not game to play with...I guess because we parents are too busy looking on FB to see how many people like the picture of their dog of family...because we don't have time to teach our children, right? Do you know someone who is like the snake (The Devil) in the Bible who tells you go ahead and do what you want regardless of what God says? Could they be on the television, on social media, a judge, or a politician??? Or do you know someone who is like a wolf in sheep's clothing who is just ready to uncover themselves and eat you for dinner because you were naive enough to get close to them? Or, do you know someone who is in your own home who is waiting for you in your bed to tell you lies, to lead you astray, or make you feel afraid of their actions? Who and what you listen to is important! And what you do and how you respond to evil (lies) is important. Your response has personal consequences for just not for you either[41]... Adam and Eve were punished together in their sin. Man will live or die (most likely together in couples bound as one) on how they live according to their actions based on how they handle deceit packaged with the Devil's lies.[42] Watch out who or where you get your information from, and who you bind yourself to.[43]

...Think about it.

---

[40] I Peter 5:8
[41] I Corinthians 10:13
[42] Ephesians 6:12
[43] James 4:7

Brian Smith

The Believer

When I was a young Christian, I was confused about something which I had learned concerning being a "Believer". I heard my mother talk about God…saying this and that. And then, I heard my father talk about Jesus…saying this and that. Both of them took me to a nice church with nice people and I heard about both God and Jesus…saying this and that. Then, I went to different churches as I grew older, and I heard messages on living a good and faithful Christian Life…on this and that. As I matured, I began comparing everything I had heard so I listened to different opinions from different Christians from all ages and walks of life on how to be a defined Christian…on this and that. And even today I still hear a myriad of opinions about Christianity and which is the correct denomination…regarding this and that, but who is right and who is not?

Jesus said beware of false prophets,[44] whether they are standing on a stage, on a street corner, or by coffee machine or a water cooler. I believe when someone either indulges others into their own mortal knowledge without a clear divine wisdom of the exact written word from either the Old testament based on God's history (and God's Law), or Jesus' grace and mercy being the Son of God as well as being the "New Covenant" (and the New Law) …where do we find our peace, understanding, and enlightenment in a diversified world of so many opinions? There is only one way: in prayer and relationship with the third entity and equal power of God Himself who is The Holy Spirit, the Great Advocate and Christian Counselor[45]…Sorry, folks, I believe when any person (anyone)

---

[44] Matthew 7:15
[45] John 14:26

Life Applications of the Holy Spirit

begins to go down the road of… this and that… about God and/or Jesus without the Holy Spirit…they are living in the world of "Man-speak" and they lose all value in their words and communication because they are not in the world of "God-Speak". It is true…. The Holy Spirit allows us to use "Man-Speak" to exist and to separate those who "Believe", and those who are "Believers". Do not be confused about this serious point. A person who believes that Jesus existed, or that He died for our sins, or is the Pathway to Heaven, is not the same as a person who has asked Jesus to take control of his or her life, and has asked Him personally into his or her heart, and then lives every moment with God in the ways of the Holy Spirit guiding them in all things.

So… one who "Believes" is not the equal as one who is a "Believer", and oh, can be even the contrary… Here is your proof. You see that Saul "believed" there existed a person named Jesus who existed, but wished he did not. He believed Jesus was a disrupter to the world and to Saul's world also, and that Jesus was evil as a disrupter, so he, Saul in his belief, persecuted those who were "True Believers" because they were disrupters as well. Saul actively rounded up and killed all "True Believers" he possibly could, but then he himself turned from "Belief in Jesus" to being a "True Believer of Jesus", and the definition happened when he was born again. The same thing happens today. After Saul met Jesus at a personal level, a "NEW Paul" then walked with the Holy Spirit with every step the rest of his life and he said… "Jesus Christ came into the world to save sinners, of whom I am the chief"[46], and ever thenceforth for those who accept Him receive "the fruit of the Holy Spirit which is love, joy, peace, patience, kindness, goodness, faithfulness, gentleness, and self-control."[47] So, the answer is you will know them by their fruit.

Do you know someone today who "Believes", but is not a "Believer"? Do you possess and show to others all nine of these fruit characteristics in your life today? This fruit outlasts today and

---

[46] I Timothy 1:15
[47] Galatians 5:22-23

passes with you into eternity. Are you truly fearful of dying? Do you hold on to things that never last?

If you are not a "True Believer", you won't possess all nine of the fruit unless you are walking with the Holy Spirit daily, and let others will see you as you are. So, which of the two believers are will you be: Saul or Paul? Have you received all nine blessings of the Fruit of the Spirit in your life? Which fruit or blessing are you missing if any? And why are you missing it?

…Think about it.

The Invitation

Every belief you believe as well as you own (good or bad) began first as a message to you from somewhere, and every message directly or indirectly started with a messenger. There are no exceptions. The message you now own could maybe have not been directed to you, but you received it anyway as an action or reaction to an action by an angel either a good or bad angel because they both exist[48].

Or, perhaps the message which stuck could have come from a troubled mother, a saintly father, a confused uncle, or misled aunt… or a bathroom wall, a beggar on the street, a mislead clergy, a student or teacher, a leader or zealot, a farmer or lawyer, etc..… A message can come in the way of pornography, or souring relationships, from indoctrination into a political group, or from reading a book on self-help, or listening to a speech from someone who seems to know something you don't. Messages can come from body language, bed-time stories, rolling of the eyes, non-participation in events or participation in events, etc..… the list of messages and how we receive them is endless. And the messages given out are given by everyone (mostly in good faith, but only two messages (or groups of messages) ever make it into the messaging "Hall of Fame" or "Hall of Shame". But the only true and valuable messages of any lasting worth are the messages given out by God, in His Triune of power: Father, Son, and Holy Ghost.

The Bible ends with the bold and inviting message in the Book of Revelation in the last chapter with Jesus's promise to return.

---

[48] Revelation 12:7

Jesus says, "Look, I am coming soon! My reward is with me, and I will give to each person according to what they have done. I am the Alpha and the Omega, the First and the Last, the Beginning and the End."

"Blessed are those who wash their robes, that they may have the right to the tree of life and may go through the gates into the city. Outside are the dogs, those who practice magic arts, the sexually immoral, the murderers, the idolaters and everyone who loves and practices falsehood.

"I, Jesus, have sent my angel to give you this testimony for the churches. I am the Root and the Offspring of David, and the bright Morning Star."

The Spirit and the bride say, "Come!" And let the one who hears say, "Come!" Let the one who is thirsty come; and let the one who wishes take the free gift of the water of life."[49]

It is truly a free gift, by just saying yes and "I am all in forever" …what do you have to lose?

…Think about it.

---

[49] Revelation 22:12-17

Life Applications of the Holy Spirit

The Cool-Aid

The older I get, the more convinced I am there are only two kinds of people in the world...Those who want fruit...and those who want Cool-Aid. Fruit is something which is grown from the ground, and created by God. It has human value in nutrition, and natural vitamins that it possesses. It has to be planted, maintained, watered, pruned, harvested, and then re-seeded for the next crop for the next crop to grow. Cool-Aid is man-made sugary drink of flavorings without nutrition. There is no connectivity or circle of life in Cool-Aid. It is but another temporary substitution for gratification in life.

Most people are not old enough to have ever heard the phrase, "Don't drink the cool-aid!" as a social warning? I remember the lesson well. The phrase originates from events in Jonestown, Guyana, on November 18, 1978, in which over 900 members of the Peoples Temple movement died. As a young boy, I remember seeing the pictures of all the dead bodies lying side by side after drinking the cool-aid that Jim Jones had his follower's drink. There was even a US Congressman who was killed in the event when he went to inspect. It was the largest loss of orchestrated civilian American life up until the events of September 11, 2001 happened. It was orchestrated by Jim Jones and his close entourage. He called his cause: "Revolutionary Suicide" when he put cyanide in the followers cool-aid and then had the members drink it, and they did. History will repeat itself so we must always keep our guard up and choose our leaders well, people not by their words, but by their fruit led by the Holy Ghost.

Jesus taught us the important lesson on who to listen to in life concerning this type of even when He said, "Watch out for false prophets. They come to you in sheep's clothing, but inwardly they are ferocious wolves. By their fruit you will recognize them. Do people pick grapes from thorn-bushes, or figs from thistles? Likewise, every good tree bears good fruit, but a bad tree bears bad fruit. A good tree cannot bear bad fruit, and a bad tree cannot bear good fruit. Every tree that does not bear good fruit is cut down and thrown into the fire. Thus, by their fruit you will recognize them."[50]

So, who are you following today to give you advice, and will following them give you good nutrition or temporary relief??? Words can be and will always twisted and used to be deceiving, to sound good to the weak and immature, but does that person have fruit to show? Do you take your financial advice from a poor person who will always be poor, or heed advice from an ill person who will always be ill? Do you take your relationship advice from someone who has a history of broken relationships? Do you take raising children and family advice from someone who has no children or family, and do you seek Godly council from someone who doesn't not know God (but he or she thinks they do), or lives in a state of Hell which is seen outwardly as well as inwardly by others, but not themselves?

If you want to know the blessings of living a Christian life, then you should seek out someone who knows the Lord, measure their fruit which they have, and then ask them to raise you up in your spiritual life so that will have nutrition and spiritual fruit too. The alternative choices usually end up having entirely atrocious bad endings.

...Think about it.

---

[50] Matthew 7:15-20

Life Applications of the Holy Spirit

The Baker's Message

Have you ever heard parents the saying to their children, "'Well maybe you can cook, but you can't bake' Or… 'Too many chefs in the kitchen never get anything done'"?

So, what does this really mean? And what weight does the experience of being a lead teacher mean?

Anyone can cook, but it takes, wisdom, teaching and skill to be a good baker. Because if you just toss anything into a pot, and add heat, it will cook; but in order to bake, you have to prepare, actively go out and purchase or make the ingredients, know the amounts going to be used, know the exact ingredients, the exact times to let things rise, and the exact temperature and times to apply the heat, and the time to let things cool before adding any extras on top.

And the perfect baker who is a purist will make his or her own butter, harvest their own wheat, grind their own grain, own their own chicken, gather the wood to make their own and build their own oven or kiln to make their own food, and ask or need no one to make the perfect baked food.

Jesus teaches all who will listen on how to be a good baker in His miracle of feeding of five thousand of His followers with just five loaves of bread and two small fish. Jesus says to His disciples…. "Very truly I tell you, you are looking for me, not because you saw the signs, I performed but because you ate the loaves and had your fill. Do not work for food that spoils, but for food that endures to eternal life, which the Son of Man will give you. For on him God the Father has placed his seal of approval."

Then they asked him, "What must we do to do the works God requires?"

Jesus answered, "The work of God is this: to believe in the one he has sent."

So, they asked him, "What sign then will you give that we may see it and believe you? What will you do? Our ancestors ate the manna in the wilderness; as it is written: 'He gave them bread from heaven to eat.'"

Jesus said to them, "Very truly I tell you, it is not Moses who has given you the bread from heaven, but it is My Father who gives you the true bread from heaven. For the bread of God is the bread that comes down from heaven and gives life to the world."

"Sir," they said, "always give us this bread."

Then Jesus declared, "I am the bread of life. Whoever comes to me will never go hungry, and whoever believes in me will never be thirsty. But as I told you, you have seen me and still you do not believe. All those the Father gives me will come to me, and whoever comes to me I will never drive away. For I have come down from heaven not to do my will but to do the will of him who sent me. And this is the will of him who sent me, that I shall lose none of all those he has given me, but raise them up at the last day. For my Father's will is that everyone who looks to the Son and believes in him shall have eternal life, and I will raise them up at the last day."

At this the Jews there began to grumble about him because he said, "I am the bread that came down from heaven." They said, "Is this not Jesus, the son of Joseph, whose father and mother we know? How can he now say, 'I came down from heaven'?"

"Stop grumbling among yourselves," Jesus answered. "No one can come to me unless the Father who sent me draws them, and I will raise them up at the last day. It is written in the Prophets: 'They will all be taught by God.' Everyone who has heard the Father and learned from him comes to me. No one has seen the Father except the one who is from God; only he has seen the Father. Very truly I tell you, the one who believes has eternal life. I am the bread of life. Your ancestors ate the manna in the wilderness, yet they died. But here is the bread that comes down from heaven, which anyone may

Life Applications of the Holy Spirit

eat and not die. I am the living bread that came down from heaven. Whoever eats this bread will live forever."[51]

So, this coming "Thanksgiving Day" … Will you truly give thanks, and understand that there is only one perfect chef in the world, and no matter how good your food that you cooked and tastes, it won't get you into Heaven or give you "Eternal Life"; only temporary pleasure.

...Think about it.

---

[51] John 6:27-51

Brian Smith

The Relatives

Have you ever thought about if you could possibly be related to Jesus through the descendants of his brothers and sisters through Mary, the mother of Our Savior? Well, somebody somewhere is genetically related to Him today... well, perhaps if any of Mary's other children ever married, had children, and their decedents are still around. I wonder if one of the fancy DNA tests today could tell us if we will ever be able to go that far back, and come up with a Mary/Jesus ancestry line...but really... who cares?

In Matthew 12, Jesus broke all blood line priorities and lineage importance! No more could people put emphasis on their DNA value or ancestry for lineage! So, if you are going to order a DNA test in the future to find out your importance or worth, don't bother...it is a just waste of hard-earned money! Everyone is important to god without favoritism, if you understand the rules. Here is why...

The truth found in Matthew 12 teaches us while Jesus was still talking to the crowd, his mother and brothers stood outside, wanting to speak to him. Someone told him, "Your mother and brothers are standing outside, wanting to speak to you." Christ, The Lord, replied to him, "Who is my mother, and who are my brothers?" Pointing to his disciples, he said, "Here are my mother and my brothers. For whoever does the will of my Father in heaven is my brother and sister and mother."[52]

From this point on in history, it is through the spirit of The Lord and not the flesh of man, that the family connection is made. All fleshly connotations are secondary in our lives, with of little or no

---

[52] Matthew 12:47-50

Life Applications of the Holy Spirit

importance, except for unbelievers who "pick and quarrel" about it like low swine in a swine trough fighting over slop they are fed to keep them fat and happy.

If anyone today says today that they are to be mature in their Christian faith and walk as it will claim, then they must claim the Spirit of Christ in their heart wholly (and consult the Holy Ghost constantly in prayer) and leave their fleshly lives behind. They must fundamentally understand this specific passage and follow the Word of God, which says "Those who belong to Christ Jesus have crucified the flesh with its passions and desires. Since we live by the Spirit, let us keep in step with the Spirit. Let us not become conceited, provoking and envying each other."[53]

So, today if you are a proponent of any particular crusade for any particular race or DNA related stature... THEN STOP! You are putting yourself above others, and you not living in the Spirit of Christ but in the Flesh of Man. The flesh of Man has little value to God the Father who controls all eternity. All flesh will dissolve one day... and the only thing left will be one's spirit to live on. Focus on these things today and pray for forgiveness you may need yourself, and you will forget the worries of the secular world tomorrow.

...Think about it.

---

[53] Galatians 5" 24-26

Brian Smith

Your Thoughts

As I have matured, I remember the things my mother taught me while growing up. She was a good woman and she taught me that the essence of all things (good and bad) first dwell in the hearts and minds of whom people really are as they speak and become what their hearts are already, either hardened or softened. So, beware whoever you listen to or get advice from; for not everyone is who they purport to be!

My mother taught me, that if a person dwells on the issue of race, then THEY are surely a racist; for no others are thinking these thoughts in the same way. And if a person dwells on the meaning of lies all the time, then surely, THEY are a lair; for these things regarding lies stand firm and preeminent in their ways which will show up. If a person dwells on stealing, then THEY must be a thief, because thievery is sewn into their soul so that it has them feeling guilty of some past action they are trying to avoid. These are the applications of words of evil people which infect others and by what men will be judged upon after that are gone to the next world. And my mother taught me lastly, that if a person dwells on love, then THEY are only a lover. They can neither hate nor anger because only love is where the heart can find its peace and cast out all other thoughts from inside. For in the heart is where people are re-born and live life as it is meant to be, and find a Savior who loves and is not filled with hypocrisy.

Hypocrisy is a favorite way of Satan, vipers, wolves, and pagans to seek out and destroy others who don't agree, always looking for their next pray who is weak, untaught, or immature. These people use their words to justify their unclean human hearts. For Jesus taught much about being a hypocrite.... In Matthew Jesus taught us

Life Applications of the Holy Spirit

from the sermon on the Mount to avoid hypocrisy when he said "Thou hypocrite, first cast out the beam log in thine own eye; then thou see clearly to cast out the mote out of thy brother's eye"[54]....and then later in Matthew, He taught us something which should be clearly preyed upon before posting on social media or speaking in public on judging others which is "Woe to you, teachers of the law, you hypocrites! You clean the outside of the cup and dish, but inside you are full of greed and self-indulgence. Blind Pharisee! First clean the inside of the cup and dish, and then the outside also will be clean."[55].... Think about hypocrisy for just a moment, and see if the shoe fits. It should not.

    ...Think about it.

---

[54] Matthew 7:5
[55] Matthew 23:25-26

Brian Smith

The Trinity

You might have asked yourself, "Does God ever change His mind?" or, "How can the Old-Testament and the New-Testament be so different and still be the same God on important issues like events going on today?" or, "Is the Bible outdated and need to be updated?" or, "How can so many people have such different opinions which are incongruent and we have so many different denominations of churches, after everyone studying the same Bible, that things can become so polarized and chaotic in definition?" Maybe because the Bible has so many translations created by the Holy Spirit that it has become fluid like the blood of Christ to meet the needs of all peoples where they are, in their time of need, and in the time in which they are born.[56]

Each of these translational versions capture the unity of "A Three in One" Triune God in different words, and words used are that are very important and can be critical to the interpretation of the content. In all these versions, it is critical to understand that the Old-Testament and the New-Testaments are the Testaments of God (Father in Heaven), as well as Lord God in the flesh Jesus Christ (Savior to the Earth), and not the Testaments of men. The words on the pages of all these versions are the historical legacies of the lives, choices and impact of men, women and their families who lived, died and became immortalized in the testament of God's existence, power and sovereignty over all. From the beginning of any thought

---

[56] Different versions of the Bible:
KJ21,ASV,AMP,BRG,CSB,CEB,CJB,CEV,DARBY,DLNT,DRA,ERV,EHV,ESVUK,EXG,GNV,GW,GNT,HSCB,ICB,ISV,JUB,KJV,AKJV,LEB,TLB,MSG,MEV,NOG,NABRE,NASB,NCV, NET,NIRV,NIV,NKVJ,NLV,NLT,NMB,NRSV,NTE,OJB,TPT,RGT,RSV,RSVCE, VOICE,WEB,WE,WYC,YLT

Life Applications of the Holy Spirit

concluded about the Bible many people erroneously believe they are reading the testaments of men and not the testament of God. Not true!

What is true is that, you, yourself will be tested in just the same as those recounted in the Bible which will become your legacy which will carry with it your own testimony, but yours will not be written in a stand-alone book such as the Bible with in any long-lasting eternal value, unless it is written as an entry into the "Book of Life" recorded as a testimony in Heaven being a Believer on earth.[57]

God (Our Father) slew His enemies both right and left according to His Old-Testament, but then The Christ (His Son) came and He forgave His earthly enemies, and showed us a new era and way. He taught us love His loved enemies, teaching us to do the same so they might avoid the fate of eternal doom and gloom as we have…. So, who are your enemies today? Why do you have any hate in your heart? Which part of God are you choosing to follow, His New or Old Testament? And where will you find the Truth without letting the Satan in to separate you from the love of God, or each other?

The answer is the single answer established by the Trinity![58] Because men, who only study the academics, heritage, and postludes of the Bible will follow the wing of the Bible related to its origin and semantics; and they become lost without the enlightenment of the Holy Spirit's clarity.[59] Those who only study the wing of the Bible which concerns salvation with its application and definition; they become lost without the enlightenment of the message of the Holy Spirit which for all mankind. You see, the Future belongs to the Testament of The Holy Spirit. It is a claim by Him as the counselor of mankind.[60]

Without understanding of the third person of the Trinity, you can try but you be confused in weight of the roles of the two parts or wings of God, as the "Do Good" wing, and the "Do Right" wing of

---

[57] Revelation 3:5, 13:8, 20:15, 21:27
[58] Matthew 28:19
[59] John 15:26
[60] John 14:17

God the Father and God the Son; which are both one in the same along with the Holy Spirit, but are divided into three different entities.

If I gave you a visual to help you understand, it would look like this... Two extremely faithful believing men or women who are pious (but not filled by the Holy Spirit) walk deep into a densely over-grown forest without a compass (phone or GPS) to lead them out and back home again. While in the forest they get lost. Before they succumb to an unfortunate physical death, they must pray to the Holy Spirit for direction, for new wisdom and knowledge to lead them out of the forest; or their fate is the same as those men who live outside the forest without God ever being a part of their lives. It takes prayer for wisdom, for wisdom does not come by believing alone.

So, your future (and also the future of the world) lies in the Testament of the Holy Spirit and your prayer asking for wisdom and direction. Just as in the Testaments of those in the Bible, the direction and wisdom given to the world will be shown through the lives of those who pray to find their way out of the forest. The best advice for anyone who does-not know the power of Holy Spirit through prayer, is find one who does and do the same as they do and you will no longer be lost... For, any man or woman who depends on another who is not in prayer and not led faithfully by the Holy Spirit but also who takes council from him seriously and his message, they will be as lost as if in that forest of gloom and doom life; just as one who never opens a Bible and never depends on the Holy Spirit for council.[61]

...Think about it.

---

[61] I Corinthians 8:4-6

Life Applications of the Holy Spirit

Righteous Anger

I have often heard the question: "Is righteous anger, ok?" ...Or "I did something out of righteous anger, so I believe it is ok!"....

Well, righteous anger IS NOT OK... because anger cannot be broken down into different sub-types; anger is anger. Anger is a personal feeling of hurt, pain, and wanting vindication. So, when someone falsely uses the term righteous anger, they become playing God, and they are wrong....no-one be God except God Himself, and we must wait on Him to do His Justice. Human anger is just another feeling when used out of control to be harnessed when in growing in the Lord. In Paul's teachings we learn what to do with our mortal anger. "Beloved, never avenge yourselves, but leave it to the wrath of God, for it is written, "Vengeance is mine, I will repay, says the Lord."[62]

...Think about it."

---

[62] Roman 12:19

Brian Smith

Back Door

Unmet expectation is one of the most under discussed consequences or our moral existence. Most often, humans have very high expectation of something in particular that is to happen, but often an opposite result happens and then the person takes in personally are they get locked in a vicious quicksand of unfulfilled emotion. The take away from this is if you have lived awhile you soon understand that God oversees all things in His own way, and in His own time...not man's, and then life begins a three-way tug of war for the person's heart.[63]

It is like watching a lost animal who is in agony and wants to show God how smart, industrious, hard-working that he or she is, as they wish to meet with God at their mortal level and plead for the outcome of their issues… So then, he or she will go out of their home and sit on their front porch to wait for God to come and meet them so that he or she can discuss the expectation of their problems. But God never comes to their front door (or of any man's front door) as the person expects, unless there is going to be a personal struggle where the animal loses.[64]

God as He does, always chooses come through an individual's back door, because it is in in God's home that the man lives and abides, and not his own[65]; for God always remains unseen, and shows His voice only at a time when the person is not expecting. All the while, the man spends waiting, (he carries his own problems personally) the man chews on his problems and the possible answers

---

[63] Proverbs 16:9
[64] Lamentations 3:25-26
[65] Genesis 1, Jeremiah 29:11-12

Life Applications of the Holy Spirit

in expectation (like a cow will chew its cud) on how he will lobby God to help him resolve his expectations of his time; and all the while, the person's issues have gotten worse and even to the point of being out of his control.[66]

And so, during the time of his waiting, God has taken up residence in the man's home, because God first built the place where the man lives, and God will clean and sturdy the house which the man could not do. This man may believe that he has been a good steward of the house, but in reality, there is only the man's dirt and decay living in there, all the while the man has been sitting outside wasting his life away one day at a time, waiting for God to arrive as he has called and come to him.[67]

Then God subtly announces His presence from inside the man's house, softly as a whisper, and then God invites the man back inside of His House (because it was never the man's house to begin with) which The Lord God built originally to match the man's temporary worldly gifts and talents. Softly, God will knock on the door from the inside calling the man's name, so that the man knows that He is there. The man (as will all men) will hear the voice of God inside calling to him from inside the house, knowing that all the while he has been outside searching to fulfill his own expectations, while God is inside, in the house living there; so that the man will have to choose to either go back inside the house and live under the rules of God and abide with Him, or he will stay outside the house which God built, without God in his life, abiding in a life without the blessings of God in his future.[68]

The choice is always up to mortal for when the man will knock back on the door as a sign, so that the door can be opened for him that he can pass back inside; and whether God's enlightenment will come to the man to address his problems and his pain (imbued by his ego), which the man loves so much and wishes to retain as a king on his own front porch of nowhere, he will remain eternally frustrated and going nowhere, and leading a life of incorrect expectations, and

---

[66] Proverbs 27:1
[67] 2 Peter 3:8-9
[68] Ecclesiastes 3:1

then leading his family on a journey which also leads them to nowhere as well.[69]

...Think about it.

---

[69] Numbers 14:18

Life Applications of the Holy Spirit

Singleness

Most everyone has heard of the "Parable of the Good Samaritan".[70] Have you? If you have, let's look closely and study who and what Jesus referenced as "Good" in this parable. But first note that the first two passers-by were members of larger groups.

The first passer-by was a priest. The larger group he was part of experienced him as doing sacrificial offerings at daily and holiday events. The second person a Levite. The larger group he was part of experienced him as providing political education to a larger body. Both of these men had their reputations to protect when they were out in public because they were beholding to their groups.... In Jesus message I believe neither of these two individuals stopped to help in the parable because of personal ties to group influence. The third person was a Samaritan, who was an individual, not tied to a group, and his only designated by a geographic place (Samaria). Though he was not from the area, he was independent from ties to others, and free to do has his heart convicted him, and also, he could do "good" for his fellow man ....

So, it was an individual by personal choice and not forced by government or groups, who had a softened heart, and who stopped gave from his own means that made an impact which Jesus taught as one doing "good" when the others who were part of groups were unable to do the same. In this parable the individual, "The Good Samaritan", did not stop to take time to think about what a group would think about his actions, or if he would be judged by others in helping a victim (what-ever his lot). This person is defined as an individual giver. This person reacted immediately through his own

---

[70] Luke 10:25-37

compassion and did not get any friends involved, or ask to raise money for the victim; he did everything by his own hands and his own resources and he did not ask anything from others in return except the aid of a healer whom he paid directly. And he was not looking for any glory or fame for his actions.

So, next time you see a person in a group trying to do the "Good thing", think about who Jesus spoke highly of in this parable to see if there in another individual who might come around later, and do the "good" thing once the multitudes in the group have left. When you look around which group are you tied to which makes you not an individual giver from the heart?

…Think about it.

Life Applications of the Holy Spirit

The Kneel

What is more important?... "To take one-knee for the temporary, or to take two-knees for the eternal?" We can see it every day around us.

Some people in this world live in self-aggrandizement and grandeur, and some do not. The world has always been defined by these two groups of two different peoples (while race has absolutely nothing to do with it).

There are those who take two knees to thank God and who are obedient to His will, and there are those who only think of themselves and not Thanking God before they kneel and take only one knee at a time (it can be for money, self-esteem, politics, wealth, identity, family, honor, respect, power, greed, love, sex, children, self-aggrandizement, looks, etc....).

The world has always been geared for the temporary... because it was designed to be temporary. And those who dwell upon it are designed to be temporary as well. Each life will be traded in exchange for something. What will your life be traded for?

Time will come and go, and we will not be able to get it back. The sun, the moon, and our creator will all be present here when all else has turned to dust, though we will not. And there will be a record of how many times a person knelt on one knee or two.

The world and its inhabitants always yearned to glorify itself by its deeds but no one in the world can take credit for even one heart beat or breath... And when the world forgets its Creator, God divorces Himself from the world. Listen to the past days of the Book of Jeremiah: "I gave faithless Israel her certificate of divorce and sent her away because of her adulteries. Because Israel's immorality mattered to her so little to her, she defiled the land and committed adultery with wood and stone."[71]

Where are you today with kneeling on two knees in thanks and prayer? I believe that just maybe for every year going forward…until we pay homage to God first in all things, the world may be going through a downward spiral. Only time can tell us because no one can see the future.

It is not my hope nor wish, but history does repeat itself. Question: Where are the past great empires that ruled the world through might and courage: Rome, Britain, Aztec, the Hun, the Dane, the Spanish, or the Portuguese, etc.… In their end, they were all consumed and destroyed from the inside outside-in.

Pick any world empire you choose to defend, but only one Empire, one Emperor, one Kingdom, one King, and one Ruler has lasted throughout the millennia; it is the Empire and King of Heaven. All others have succumbed and fallen to the ills of self-aggrandizement combined with conceit. Today I am praying on my two knees that the world will wake up to what is happening around it, so that all the prosperity and blessings which the Lord has bestowed upon it may continue; but I don't see it happening soon. The invisible plagues (selfishness, self-aggrandizement, lewdness, impure thought, sexual immorality, lack of moderation, character assassination, and verbal immaturity) are all quietly consuming the world once again like a cataclysmic nightmare growing closer to being ruled by darkness instead of light, unless we awaken and be revived like a sleeping giant and taken the world again down to the river to be baptized, redeemed, and born again into a world that knells only to God.

---

[71] Jeremiah 3:8

Life Applications of the Holy Spirit

Will you pray on two knees with me to help make this happen? God will continue to divorce Himself from His creations, as His people all only think about themselves who give little praise, gifts, and glory to Him, as our Creator, which He yearns for in His love and then gives back to us in return at least one hundred-fold[72]

…Think about it.

---
[72] Mark 10:30, Matthew 13:3-9

Brian Smith

The Name

Everyone it seems wants to be a Bible scholar, but only a few are willing to do the work. The real true of being a student of the Bible is which way to correctly say Jesus' name. A simple question, right? So, take the test...Which is most correct way to refer to Jesus, and what makes these ways different... "Jesus-Christ"[73], "Christ-Jesus[74]", or "Jesus - The Christ[75]"? These are commonly all used interchangeably. But, are they all the same??? The answer is no...

The word "Christ" comes from the Greek word meaning "The Anointed One". But also, in the Greek Septuagint, it come from the Hebrew meaning "Messiah". All those who have been sitting in church services as children and listening as vessels to be filled, should remember the lesson when Jesus asked his disciples, "Who do they say The Son of Man is?"[76] Then Simon Peter (A Hebrew) answers, "You are THE CHRIST. So, Peter was the first Jew (of which was the chosen people)[77]on record who acknowledged Him as The Messiah, "The Son of the Living God".

This begins the Messianic Message ripple effect that lasts still today because only True Believers believe that Jesus is the True Messiah. Those who are consider themselves as ~partial 2% believers, or ~30% believers or even ~e75%, etc.... e.g., those who think Jesus was perhaps just another Old Testament prophet, or just a really good person with a really good message all about love and

---

[73] Matthew 1:1
[74] Romans 3:24, 8:2, 8:39, 16:3, I Corinthians 1:2, 1:30, II Corinthians 4:5
[75] Matthew 16:20
[76] Mathew 16:16
[77] Deuteronomy 14:2

Life Applications of the Holy Spirit

forgiveness he was willing to die for, but certainly not The Messiah, no never! For them, this just can't be true; it is impossible, just too weird and too far out of reach to believe in, as so say some, but true believers will not be ever erased from historical records, so the belief lives on.

Then to add "The Messiah" definition, the term Christ is defined in Greek as "The Anointed", so Jesus Christ, really translates to the title of "Jesus- The Messiah & Anointed One". But anointed by whom?....God in Heaven? This can be confusing because we are told that Jesus is God in human flesh. So, how was Jesus anointed? By whom? The Hebrews refer to "being anointed" with Holy oil, but Jesus was referred to as being anointed by the Holy Spirit when he was baptized. The Bible recounts that, "When Jesus went up out of the water, at that moment, Heaven was opened, and He saw the Spirit of God descending like a dove and alighting on Him".[78] Then it was when He received his anointing from His Father in Heaven.

Then what about the difference when referring to "Jesus Christ" as "Christ Jesus"? In His day, not everyone was given last names yet, only first names. A person might have title like King, Governor, Praetor, Dominus, General, Centurion, etc.… So, Christ Jesus is actually a distinguishment, like Pope is to John Paul, or King to Henry, or General to Eisenhower, etc.… So, Christ Jesus is a proper title of the highest ranking being: "The Anointed One: Jesus", and this highest title without the Holy oil from Jewish priests being applied by the Hebrew law really hacked allot of the legal hierarchy off, and those with lesser titles were quite unhappy with their demotions. Of course, no one had any legal standing to do anything about it because Jesus never hurt anyone, so the only charge they could use was trumped up blasphemy (i.e., no freedom of speech).

So, which term when referring to Jesus is best used when? …When you say Jesus-Christ, you are calling him anointed; when you say Christ-Jesus, you are giving Him title status over all others; and when you call Him Jesus-The Christ, you are saying He is the Messiah. So, as you might already know, Jesus-Christ Christ is the most commonly used term today because since He was anointed by

---

[78] Matthew 3:16

the Holy Spirit, all the believers in Jesus Christ share in the anointment by the same Holy Spirit. And that is why these people are called Christians, anointed to live differently, by the Holy Spirit. Being a Christian is not a term to be taken lightly because of the life commitment, which is to live by a higher moral and ethical code, and to be different from the crowd in a blessed way… So, if you are a true Believer, and you have been baptized, you have been anointed too by the Holy Spirit, just Like Jesus. If you haven't, then maybe you should consider making a change for your own sake.

…Think about it.

Life Applications of the Holy Spirit

Blended Family

Are you aware that Jesus lived in a "Blended Family"? It is true... Jesus did not have a nuclear family. His father, Joseph, was not his biologic dad, because Jesus only had a biologic mortal mother. Joseph was a step-father, a step-dad. Joseph and Mary two were the perfectly chosen parents for God's Son, Jesus "The Christ" on earth, as a mother and step-father. So, before any wise-guys start in on who the family legitimately was according to which version of Bible we are referring to and if they really were really real parents.... In the King James version (a Protestant version), the Gospel of Mark (6:3) and the Gospel of Matthew (13:55-56) mention James, Joseph (Joses), Judas (Jude) and Simon as bothers of Jesus, the son of Mary. The same verses also mention unnamed sisters of Jesus. Mark (3:31-32) tells us about Jesus' mother and brothers looking for Jesus. So, they are real!

The Bible is a well written and accurate history book as well as inspired Truth that has lasted through the ages, so anyone who wishes to take on the Bible and its 2000-year record, can do it please in another person's post. Thank you...What I wanted to think about was how the perfect step dad, Joseph, must have struggled when he communicated with his step family as the leader of the house (please study more if you object). Do you think there was 100% harmony in that family or possibly maybe any family dissension there? And do you think that maybe Joseph and Mary had some long family meetings on how to best run the house when their oldest child was different from the rest? Was Jesus treated differently? ... I can almost imagine the other children (boys and girls) questioning their parents at bed time, "Dad, tell us again about when Jesus was born...Mom, did really three kings show up and bring him gift from afar? Was there really a big humongous star outside that showed the kings and their caravan, and the shepherds, the way to Bethlehem and the birth? Why was the King so mad that our brother (i.e. Jesus in our Christian Step family) was born that afterwards he ordered all the baby boys killed in the city, and then you and mommy had to run to Egypt to save you lives, because God told you to go? Now your question: Why do you think Jesus asked total strangers to be his disciples instead of his brothers and sisters? Don't you think His brothers and/ or sisters were close to Him, and that He would include them in His closest circle? Even in His close family in Heaven? Well, shucks, there is God's perfect answer in Matthew 12:46-50: 46 While Jesus was still talking to the crowd, his mother and brothers stood outside, wanting to speak to him. 47 Someone told him, "Your mother and brothers are standing outside, wanting to speak to you." 48 He replied to him, "Who is my mother, and who are my brothers?" 49 Pointing to his disciples, he said, "Here are my mother and my brothers. 50 For whoever does the will of my Father in heaven is my brother and sister and mother." Now here is today's question, "ARE YOU... doing the will of your Father in Heaven today with your life? Or are you too busy doing the will of yourself here on earth? The question is the same after 2000 years. When Jesus said these things to His disciples (with family outside), it is what most people would call an insult to His family, but to the rest of the world it was a new invitation, an unfulfilled blessing! It was the greatest invitation to the greatest event ever in the history of the world! So, do you understand that the family of Christ is just one big "Blended Family" in Heaven and here on earth? No-one gets in by already being in, or marries in, or is born in, or gets a special pass to get in... you and everyone must to choose to be in! The blood lines do not matter, Jesus was a Jew, and he broke the promise of ancestral lineage in one simple verse. The message is we all have different mothers and fathers here on earth, but we have the same Father in Heaven just like Jesus if we choose Him! So, if you think about it, we are all just like his biologic brothers and sisters in his original blended family. Not only was Jesus a step brother to them then, but He was also their Lord and Savior within their family lives too! His step brother, James, is given credit later to writing the Book of

Life Applications of the Holy Spirit

James, and His brother Judas (not the same as the disciple Judas) is given credit later for possibly writing the Book of Jude. How cool is that! I hope this gives you some more insight into the words of their two books called James and Jude next time you pick up a Bible and read from it.

...Think about it.

Brian Smith

The Teachers

I would like to take a moment to salute many of the wonderful academic teachers who shaped our lives. The four most outstanding high school teachers I remember (after all these years) are Shirley Hofland, Mr. McClure, Bryan Adams, and Mr. Gill.

Shirley Hofland taught me how to think outside of the box when everyone else painfully lived and thought inside of boxes as they do still today. Mr. McClure taught me how to think using the geometric and algebraic building blocks of mathematics which I later came to understand controlled the elements of music, poetry, and statistics. Bryan Adams taught me how to have fun in life by being a student of life, as he many times stood upon tables as he taught hovering over us to keep our attention, and Mr. Gill taught me the importance of probability. With those basic core principles my parents then took me to church on Sundays to learn values, so I learned about fellowship, humility, social importance, and serving from the heart, not the pocket book. The church was called the People's Church because that is just what it was, the People's Church. A non-denominational church of believers who shared their lives together. There were no airs or egos in the body of the church; just good people who were grateful for their lives and being healthy and literate. I used the core principles we all learned in school and applied them in life and vice versa; and they still apply today. The people who did not go to church on Sundays I later learned, thought by doing so, they were more-free than the church goers by not encumbering their time, when really, they were not free at all. I learned that the laws of the world we live in like physics, algebra, and mathematics were tools of intellectuals to fool themselves into thinking that they were greater than they really were by only living

Life Applications of the Holy Spirit

for themselves, and in reality, all that intellectualism gained them nothing more than a few dollars and a place in the graveyard in the end.

    I remember my football coach Carlos Vela said to me in middle school.... "Never out run your punt coverage", and that application has helped me tremendously in my Christian walk.[79] Regarding statistics, I learned that if we believe in Jesus as our Lord and Savior, we have a 100% chance of going to Heaven.[80] I always like receiving 100% of a good thing. How about you? Unfortunately, Jesus also said that those who don't believe in Him have a high chance of not getting into Heaven... Is it 100%, maybe? None of us know on this day, but I don't want to chance it... So, I am going to continue being a believer until the very end. All others can choose their probability and statistics as they want. Thank you, Mr. Gill and all the others!

    ...Think about it.

---

[79] I Thessalonians 2:12, Colossians 2:6
[80] I John 2:1-29, John 3:36

Brian Smith

All Lives Matter

The message of Jesus Christ is "All lives matter [period].[81]" Do not be deceived in any other feel-good watered-down or self-centered-versions you hear because Jesus' message has withstood all tests of time that "All lives matter". Jesus did not say that anyone had more privilege or was more important than another.[82] This goes for all, not just those who believe they have been victimized. All other messages are just seasonal. For whoever believes that they have been mistreated and mistreats another is sinning against God.[83] The message then has been twisted for self-gain and is doing evil against his neighbor for self-gain. And those who promote a twisted message of the day with contempt in their heart will be judged accordingly. This includes anyone and all who believes in creating one victim to save another is ok. These do-gooders will only do for themselves in their selfishness like the flavor of the day or wolf in sheep's clothing.[84] Other messages never last. Only Jesus' messages last, and only God in Heaven is good, no others are.[85] No-one else except the Son of God could have taken what he took preaching His message that "All Lives Matter" in His day saying that...Not just Roman's lives mattered, but All lives mattered...not just Hebrew's or Gentile's lives mattered, but All lives mattered, not just master's or slave's lives mattered, but All lives mattered, and not any single sect, creed, color, or gender mattered more than the other.

---

[81] Parable of the Lost Sheep: Matthew 18:12-14, Luke 15:3-7
[82] Matthew 7:5
[83] Matthew 25:14-30
[84] Matthew 7:15
[85] Mark 10:10

Life Applications of the Holy Spirit

God Himself was willing to die on the cross for us and for us to spread that He loves the whole world as His creation, and not just parts of it.[86] All lives matter to Jesus unconditionally![87] Please be clear, His message was clear: "All Lives Matter." And because of this message, all colors of all people born in the past or in the future will be included in Heaven, and none withheld or held back, for those who believe in Him and are obedient in His commands.[88] And those who will be excluded will be those who do not believe in Him, and do not follow His commands[89]; which was also His message, not ours. So, what is more important: the message of the eternal or the message of the temporary??? Anyone who says anytime that one certain group matters more than another group and gives their message outside of the Truth of Christ's love, and is separate and wrong from the message of Jesus Christ that "All Lives matter". These are not speaking with a heart for Jesus and a message of inclusion (so beware). They are false prophets in sheep's clothing. Their lips and actions are not speaking for God, and their words will fade like the wind on a hot summer's day, with lips that deceive and others to follow in unrighteousness....and this is not a good message for them, you, your children, or the world. All twisted messages are only temporary like hard fought riches that never last.[90]

...Think about it.

---

[86] John 3:16
[87] Luke 15:8-10
[88] Luke 23:43
[89] 1 Corinthians 6:9-11
[90] Matthew 6:19-20

Brian Smith

Parental Lies

All parents and grandparents please listen… the act of lying always comes back to roost at home and returns to hurt the most cherished loved ones close to you. Lies don't have to be from just one person. They can come inherently from a group, a culture, a family, a political party, or millions of other sources… and when it happens, it eventually hurts everyone involved sooner or later with a ripple effect that outlasts the person or people who were a part of it.[91]

But everyone lives somewhat of a lie, don't we? So, why do we judge others harshly without judging ourselves first??? None of us is perfect, except God, but why do we continue to lie when it is not necessary just because we like to lie, just like Satan likes to lie? He is the King of telling non-truths. Lies serve no-one, so why do we do it? God commanded us to, "Thou shalt not lie[92]", so why do we constantly do it? Stop it!

We all know that the most pervasive three lies in America we tell our children today are Santa Claus, The Easter Bunny, The Tooth Fairy.

Most will say, "Oh, come on now friend, you are being too cold and heartless when you say that", but what about lies in politics? Lies in the media? Lies by spinning the truth at work or at home? Is this not the same as the lies told as children just to have a little fun? Now, just hold that thought…).

---

[91] Deuteronomy 5:9m
[92] Leviticus 19:11

Life Applications of the Holy Spirit

Most of us would say these three lies are only "little white lies", and they are just fine because they really don't mean anything of significance. Really? And lying to children has no consequences? Children grow up to become adults and these are the standards they are taught to live by.

The birth of Jesus, God Incarnate, who came to love everyone unconditionally and save the world was murdered and tortured, for loving everyone in the word. He came and proclaimed, "I am the Truth, The Way, and the Life", to have salvation through grave and mercy but His message is reduced by parental spewed white lies about a fictitious little man who flies around in a sleigh pulled by flying reindeer, then comes down the chimney and brings children presents just for "being good"'. That is not the message of salvation. It is just another distraction leading to hell. Ok, well, then, about three months later, is The Easter Bunny lie shows up. This prevalent parental lie shows up on the same day of The Lord's Resurrection[93], the most important day in all of history; and the day is tainted by another little white lie so parents can feel good giving children candy hidden in the yard, placed in eggs, laid by a mythical bunny that will rot their teeth out just for "being good". Why not we just leave it a religious holiday, and get rid of the lying and mixed messages and leave it about salvation?[94]…Then some eggs have money too for "being good". So, now for the all-grown-up children who were told all these lies, Uncle Sam has become the Easter Bunny for adults who are still living in their childhood, and want free government candy for just "being good" adults… Who is going to pay for the free candy? Guess who… your children! Once again lesson number two is teaching our children that lying is ok, and now it has backfired on you.

Then, the Tooth Fairy lie is spewed around about age 6 comes to our children, usually after they have figured out that Santa and The Easter Bunny are huge parental lies, but wink, wink the parents do it again! This lie shows up to give our children money or presents again, but this under their pillows for just "being good". For a third

---

[93] John 11:25-26
[94] Romans 10:9

time a new culture of children has been lied to by their parents who are the ones they should trust the most, no wonder the culture has so many problems with telling the truth and living in the light of Jesus…Can you see where we are going with this? The culture is damned from the lies the parents promote to children in good faith, but they are still lying. The culture is no better and just as sinful as any other culture that does other atrocities for which this culture condemns.

Then, many parents lie when they get married and then divorce tearing apart the children, and not honor their wedding vows, for better or worse, and the kids see them as hypocrites one more time, getting hurt the most, especially if the marry over and over again, each time saying "I do" but it means nothing in front of the children. I think the children are getting smarter and the parents are getting dumber with each generation, because there is no cure for vaccine discovered for hypocrisy combined with lying, other than common sense; and this is something our whole country is lacking today: very little to no common sense at all.

This year, please do not continue to lie to your children about these Goof balls: Santa Clause, The Easter Bunny, the Tooth Fairy? If you do, you will promote that lying is perfectly and then wonder why the culture stinks all around you. No wonder there is so much discourse and distrust in our society because of the inane personal hypocrisy which has become part of our cultural fabric from the brunt of lying. If we would simply stop all the lying and humble ourselves as a nation and also turn our country towards Jesus, (The Truth, The Way, and The Life) and turn away from hypocrisy of evil that lying befits, we might have a chance as a nation of not falling apart and losing all the good our ancestors worked for.

Life Applications of the Holy Spirit

If this path continues on the lying and dishonest course, then everyone will be a loser, where no truth can prevail outside of ourselves. The only person that we can ever effectively change is ourselves, and that is a heart change. So, I challenge everyone, if you are trying to change another person, (or group) except by serving in the Kingdom of the Lord first, I wouldn't hold your breath till you see any positive change: because it is just another moot point that has no meat on its bones.

…Think about it.

Brian Smith

The Dog Comparison

Would an individual use a team of chihuahuas to pull his or her sled and themselves in the 1161- mile Alaskan Iditarod Trail sled race in unthinkable weather? Probably not because all dogs are not the same and making discerning choices based on their gifts and talents[95] are important. Some dogs can follow a trail with a wonderful nose for smell. Some are quite athletic and can catch a Frisbee flying in the air, and others are good swimmers, and divers. Some are smarter than others being able to figuring out situations better, while some are better at obedience and not being distracted, while others…not so much. Some dogs are quite needy and want to play all day, some dogs are good for the hunt and live for the next morning run. Some dogs are good at search and recover, while some are just plain mean and incorrigible and are disrupters to the pack... Some are pedigreed and full blooded, and some are mixed genes of multiple blood lines. Some will bark all day and night and inflame the neighbors by being loud and some are quiet and never make a sound. Dogs come in all different colors, shapes, traits, and needs. From warm weather dogs, to cold weather dogs. And guess what? Dogs are a lot like people and people are a lot like dogs.

People certainly are not all the same either. They each have their own God given gifts and talents. But if a person listens to the gate keepers of dissemination with only half an ear, that person would think all people are the same. If all others are not on our guard, individuals get tricked and into thinking that people are all people the same in realm of all things, but this not true. This is wrong. People will never all be the same! Rewards will never be the same. Incentives will never be the same. Opportunities will never be the

---

[95] Matthew 22:37-40

Life Applications of the Holy Spirit

same, and life's journey will never be the same for all people…Never! The best we can do is take what comes and make lemonade from the lemons that are handed to us and not worry.[96]

It is true that leaders and followers, givers and takers, honest people and dishonest people, haters and lovers, believers and non-believers are all as different as Huskies and Chihuahuas when it comes to living with purpose and not worrying. Faith[97] is our only ray of hope we can rely on.

As mere sojourners through unmitigated life, we can never conclude that one color or breed of dogs (or race) is better than another in any way, or one blood line is better than the other; but we can say that one dog (or individual) has different or better individualized gifts and talents given to them from God above, Their Creator, to suit them (or us) in a particular task or race for working as a team or just as an individual. Jesus takes this simple Truth one step further to teach us about the next world we possible can be a part of. He speaks for God "Our Father in Heaven" when uses imagery speaking about dogs in His love and grace given to all mankind when He offers His love for all men and for women regardless of their given lot in His verbal exchange with a Canaanite woman needing help for someone else, she could not do herself and talking about dogs.[98]

The conversation went like this…. The woman came and knelt before Jesus saying to Him. "Lord, help me!" Jesus replied, "It is not right to take the children's bread (For Israel) and toss it to the dogs?" "Yes, it is, Lord," she said. "Even the dogs eat the crumbs that fall from their master's table."

Then Jesus said to her, "Woman, you have great faith! Your request is granted." And her daughter was healed at that moment.

So, like a dog, when a person of any size shape or color, gift or talent, is hungry enough, and cannot rely on their own resources to survive…will they will humble themselves enough to eat the crumbs

---

[96] Matthew 6:25-34
[97] Hebrews 11
[98] Matthew 15:25-28

of Jesus that have fallen from the table meant for others? Some may, and some not until the hunger is too much for them to endure. Some will die from starvation, too proud to eat the crumbs the master drops, and some will ask for help to live to see[99] and reap a harvest[100] for another day.

...Think about it.

---

[99] I Corinthians 13:12, 2 Corinthians 5:7
[100] Galatians 6

Life Applications of the Holy Spirit

History Lesson

Most people do not think much about the truly big historically events which are recorded in the Bible which happened except that Jesus was born[101] and then they bastardize the event by adding Santa Clause, flying rein deer and little elves making toys to the story.

About 700-800 years before the birth of Jesus were the prophets (Isaiah, Micah, Hosea, etc....); and before them was Moses and the stories of "The Burning Bush", "The parting of the Red Sea", and the "Plagues & Exodus" sending the Israelites out of Egypt and "Them wandering in the desert for 40 years".[102]

So, roughly about 3500 years ago the Bible records that God sent two men: Moses (at about age 80; speaking for God) and his brother Aaron (at about age 84; speaking as a prophet), to tell a Pharaoh, the King in charge in Egypt, Ramses II, along with his officials and his magicians to "Let My People Go" from underneath Egypt's slave drivers and its foremen setting their work schedules, so that they could "worship God in the desert". When Moses delivers God's message over and over again unsuccessfully, the Lord begins the purging of His people from the Egyptian people so that the two groups could be separated by physical definition. One would leave the other; this giving God's people freedom from bondage. But in order to accomplish this, God sends a bunch of plagues to Egypt[103]... one right after the other directed at the Egyptian people and their leadership trying to convince all of them to let God's people (which is the Egyptian slave work force) to leave.

---

[101] Luke 2
[102] Exodus 5-16
[103] Exodus 7-12

Brian Smith

This purging did not go so easily for the families involved. They ended up living in the dessert God gave them for 40 years until two generations of men died before they were set free in their new land.[104] And it was not much easier when Hebrews were purged from the believers in Jesus, across the Mediterranean Sea during the Roman Empire reign some ~1500 years later taking them to new lands away from Israel.

With Moses, God first sent miracles of His power (changing wood into snakes), then He polluted their drinking water (the Nile River), and sent animals (frogs) to inhabit their houses, sent gnats to cover their bodies, sent flies to cover the inside of their houses and cover the ground, killed their food supply by killing all their livestock so none were left, sent boils to break out on men and their animals, sent hail to destroy the crops in the field, sent locusts to consume every leaf on every tree and any food that is left, and then sent darkness so no one could see anything for three days from a total blackout. After all this, God's people still had not been allowed to leave safely and go on their own way. Then God uses his most powerful tool… He begins the death of loved ones and loved prized possessions, to sway His intentions. He breaks the dynasties that control them and He sets His will of obedience in motion.

Does history ever every repeat itself? In fact, on that day, God engineered the demise of all the firstborn sons of the Egyptians, as well as their slaves, and their cows all in a single event. The Hebrews who were spared that last horrific event celebrate it today as the "The Passover" where they were left unharmed, and then set free…well, for a while.

So, when we look at the "Big Picture" of God purging His people again, what do we all see? God is trying to free His people from current slave drivers and foreman who want people to succumb more to the country's control. Why is there so much political unrest everywhere? Do we all see so many people suffering from lives being impacted by super natural forces beyond our control? What about the impact of the exponential rising rate of children born with autism in the young boys of the nation? This is affecting more than

---

[104] Joshua 5:6

Life Applications of the Holy Spirit

just first born. America is becoming a nation of autistic, cancerous, selfish people with aging dementia who worship media idols and false Gods and have no reference for the sanctity of life through abortion and loose laws?

Could God once again be dividing us into two groups so that one group can leave the other group behind again his chosen people can migrate to another location with more of God's freedoms?

World migration has been going on since the beginning of time where groups people leave from bad situations seeking better ones and then others follow. This is the way America was founded when the Puritans left their homes Europe for the New World from under King George's dictatorship with his loyalists fighting not allowing them to leave in a war called the American Revolution; to keep their work force and control in place just like the Pharaoh in Egypt…and afterwards, who was left?... only the dead soldiers at the bottom of a separated sea or on lost battle fields and the king with his faithful loyalists (same as Ramses II and King George) who wondered what happened to their workers when God released them to leave and to seek freedom in a better location; by whatever means, the oceans parting, endless wandering in deserts, world wars or just being hungry for something different from every day provided God given manna.[105]

…Think about it.

---

[105] Exodus 16:1-36

Brian Smith

Two Enemies

When I was about 8 or 9 years old, my father sat me down at our kitchen table and asked he me a point-blank question which I will never forget…He said to me, "Son, do you know that you have two enemies?" I was stunned by his question at such a young age. And I said, "Dad, I am not even 10 years old yet. I don't even know anyone. How can I have any enemies?" I knew that my dad had served in the military, and he often commented at the kitchen table about war situations and politics; so, I thought this question mistakenly had something to do with one of these.

Then my father said to me next, "You know, we all have the same two enemies.[106] Even I have them. They are terrible enemies; horrid, and sometimes they can be uncontrollable. They have a tendency to sneak up on us when we are not thinking about them. And sometimes we just have to grab them and hold them down so they cannot get us."

At this moment, my dad reached up and grabbed his upper and lower lips and he gave them a squeeze. And, when he let them go, he said this to me, "Our worst enemies are always located here, right between our chin and our nose".

I thought to myself, ok… "So, what did I say today that caused me to get this rather blunt father-son talk; but I know now he was just taking some special time, to teach me how to live a better life for myself, and stay out of harm's way (in an unjust world). So, what did I do with his advice? As I matured, and I saw the world in action and how people spouted off their opinions with unqualified words,

---

[106] Proverbs 5:2

Life Applications of the Holy Spirit

and I began to see references in the Bible which supported my father's life long lesson to me. My father read the Bible every night so I knew he practiced what he preached to me, and he was a great man. Here are a couple of Bible verses I would like to share with you today which are a part of my father's legacy:

Whoever conceals hatred with lying lips,
and spreads slander, is a fool.[107]
Those who guard their lips preserve their lives,
but those who speak rashly will come to ruin.[108]

The mouths of fools are their undoing,
and their lips are a snare to their very lives.[109]
"Whoever would love life
and see good days
must keep their tongue from evil
and their lips from deceitful speech…[110]

…Think about it.

---

[107] Proverbs 10:18
[108] Proverbs 13:3
[109] Proverbs 18:7
[110] I Peter 3:10

Brian Smith

The Invisible World

If I put a glass of "ice-tap water" on a table with a lid covering its top, how many types of H2O would I have in the glass....1,2, or 3? If you chose 3, you get a "A" for this simple quiz, and you answer speaks volumes about your Bible IQ.

This a classic example of The Triune God, who in exists three different forms, but is all the same God as we refer to Him differently as The Father, The Son, and The Holy Ghost (Spirit) in. Is there a difference? Jesus was the physical form we could have touched in a materialistic world if we had been there two thousand years ago. In the Book of John, Jesus said, "Believe Me, that I am in the Father, and the Father is in Me.[111]" Can you see the similarity? This is like saying: you may not understand the fundamentals of biology, chemistry, physics, gravity, electrons, magnetism, cell phones, Wi-Fi, sonar, black holes, space travel, core magma, polarity, eggs and mitosis, etc...., etc....etc....but The Father and I are both intrinsically the same like H2O solid ice and H2O water vapor.

Immediately before Jesus made this statement He also stated, "If you knew the Gift of God and who it is that asks you for a drink, you would have asked him and He would have given you living water.[112]" Remember that when ice melts it transforms into its fluid state, and it becomes ubiquitous, much like the H2O water which surrounds the H2O ice in the glass. When the H2O ice melts it goes away, and only the H2O water state remains; just as when Jesus went

---

[111] John 14:11
[112] John 4:10

Life Applications of the Holy Spirit

to Heaven and He left the Holy Spirit in His place to be all around us (and in us).

And there is always some H2O that remains in the glass in all times. It is like God Himself hovering over the H2O water, and the H2O ice, constantly as the invisible H2O water vapor everywhere. H2O is even there when the ice and the water are gone in the air along with the nitrogen, oxygen, etc….. H2O is within us and fills us because we ourselves are made of water as creations (not evolution) of God. In fact, water is the one thing we need 24-7 constantly; even more than food we eat, or we will die and pass this earth, and our bones will return to the ground from which they came. Isn't chemistry class great??? And we think we all are the smart ones who figured this all out…. Well, guess what, we did not.

From the very beginning God put each of us together perfectly and the world together perfectly also. He showed us His miracles by coming here, and living with us, because He loves each of us in His Trinity-Triune state (Three in One, Father Son and Holy Ghost) and He "God" does not make any trash; in you or in the world!

And there is nothing any of us can do (as His created beings) to make this world any more perfect than it already is, (because He is in control…For in Him, in His Three worlds, He is in control at all times (not us) no matter how much we all try, think, or believe we are in control. The truth of the matter is, the more we all try to adjust and alter the nature of our Creator to make it better (for our own gain) all we do is temporarily mess things up until He fixes it again…

…Think about it.

Brian Smith

God's Timepiece

The moon is a beautiful miracle in the sky. Its moving light calendar shines bright for all to witness and see. It is God's eternal clock, a celestial pendulum in constant harmonic motion, with which He measures our time here on earth. And it is a constant reminder to us that when we look up toward Him is wonderment, we should praise Him for all He has done for us.[113] When each of us does, we comprehend and understand that not even a single mortal clock that we think we have created for our own use even matters to God, because only His clock matters to Him.

Mine eyes have witnessed this miracle perfectly with sight which God gave to me because He made it perfect in His creation as another testament for me and for you. It is in perfect harmony like He is in the skies; washing our oceans, coordination our life cycles, and shielding us apart from invading destruction like a mighty iron angel in the sky. But when I tried to capture its purpose with a common camera, it became fuzzy and unclear with my man-made lens. For the true meaning of our live is like that too.

Tomorrow, it will be the Lord's Day, because every day is the Lord's Day. The Sabbath is but just one special day to remember Him as the Lord over everything under the sun,[114] all others fall in line until the next Sabbath is begun to honor Him once again.[115]

In passing it is my hope and prayer that all those whose spent their time expounding their own mortalities on social media each day in an effort to shine their own light shine on themselves with their

---

[113] Psalm 89:37, Psalm 136:9
[114] Ecclesiastes 1:14
[115] Mark 2:27

Life Applications of the Holy Spirit

blessings or opinions for others to see, will seek out God's truth and attend a church with their families giving to receive God's message and then stand in awe of the enlightenment received, giving thanks for all the good there is around them, and let God's light shine on them so that all might witness and observe God's true love clearly from them and avoid witnessing life's fuzzy light through the lens of an imperfect world.[116]

…Think about it.

---

[116] Ephesians 2:8-9, Corinthian 5:21

Believe in Miracles

Who is still waiting for a miracle in their life? It's never too late to observe and understand those which already exist around you...

When the world and God's children begin hurting, we naturally look for miracles from above to ease our pain. But when we find none which we ask for, we become calloused and hardened with uneasy hearts because something important is still missing.... we still need to surrender....

Jesus said in the Book of John:

"If I do His work, believe in the evidence of the miraculous works I have done, even if you don't believe me. Then you will know and understand that the Father is in me, and I am in the Father."[117]

...Think about it.

---

[117] John 10:38

Life Applications of the Holy Spirit

Trap for Fools

God said in Isaiah "For my thoughts are not your thoughts, neither are your ways my ways!" declares the Lord. "As the heavens are higher than the earth, so are my ways higher than your ways and my thoughts than your thoughts.[118]

So, we must all remember these words when we think that we are doing good… but NOT seeking the Lord's will before we act, speak, or lead…, because most of the evil in the world has been done in the name of "DOING GOOD" … For man's Good intentions do not always bring about good results.[119]

The most-evil people in the world do the devil's work under the auspices of doing good because their work is outside of God's will. Be careful with the men and women you choose to follow as leaders with the good things they purport as doing good,[120] For even Jesus who conquered death, and showed his miracles to prove his divinity said…. "Why do you call ME GOOD? No one is good—except God alone.[121]"

History has proven that he or she who has a hardened heart while casting stones at one person or group while defending another, is nothing more than purporting impious sanctimony…and a trap for fools.[122]

…Think about it!

---

[118] Isaiah 55:8-9
[119] Proverbs 16:2
[120] James 4:3
[121] Mark 10:18
[122] John 8:7

Brian Smith

Worry is Useless

I had three mentors. One of them named, Bill, was a great man who had one foot that was a size seven, and one foot that was a size ten, and one of his legs was longer than the other so he had one shoe that had an extra-high sole... Bill had been infected with the polio virus when he was a child, and he was subjected as a child to a horrid treatment in an iron lung, but he had the best attitude on living I ever knew. He was an avid sailor, a Christian, and he loved the outdoors. As a teen, he told me that he had experienced an entire world which was afraid of global destruction from all out global nuclear war. "Everyone built bomb shelters in their homes," he said but it never happened. Then he explained to me the truth that "once a person becomes afraid of death, he or she is already dead."[123]

Jesus words are, "Therefore I tell you, do not worry about your life, what you will eat or drink; or about your body, what you will wear. Is not life more than food, and the body more than clothes? Look at the birds of the air; they do not sow or reap or store away in barns, and yet your heavenly Father feeds them. Are you not much more valuable than they? Can any one of you by worrying add a single hour to your life?"[124]

---

[123] James 1:17
[124] Matthew 6: 25-34

Life Applications of the Holy Spirit

The devil steals from us our happiness when we let him in our hearts[125]...how long will it take us to return to the in joy in living if we worry of dying or death coming to knock? I pray, give to God what He wants from you today,[126] so you can live in peace forever, and never fear of dying or think about death again…

...Think about it!

---

[125] I Peter 5:8
[126] I Thessalonians 5:18, Colossians 3:17, Psalm 100:1-5, Psalm 107:1

Brian Smith

Intellectualism

I met a stranger in a coffee shop who was rigorously lecturing others around him concerning his knowledge about the differences in the world, the history of religion and the downfalls of Christianity. He was quite boastful in his intellectual prowess and in the authors of all the books he had read on these subjects. He rattled off facts and figures without taking a breath...But I could tell he had an internal stench and very personal problem that was not obvious to himself, but obvious to others. [127]

So, I asked him first if I could ask him a personal question. He said yes, so I asked him, "Do believed in the Resurrection of Jesus? He answered that he was an engineer, and a scholar, and ALL things must be logical for him in order to believe in them. Then he replied following with, "I am an atheist, and 'the resurrection' is not logical."[128]

So, I then asked him a second question and that was, "if he believed in miracles, and if had he ever needed a miracle in his life but did not receive it?"... For in him, there was something obvious fueling hate and disdain for the Believers, but he could not see he was filled with hate... He said, "I do not believe in miracles, they are not logical."

So, I asked him one more question, and I said, "Do you possess any faith of any kind?" and he said, "Faith is my greatest problem. I do not have any." So, I replied for the man, whom I did not know, "I will pray for you then that when you need a miracle you will receive it, because everyone comes to a point in life where they understand

---

[127] Matthew 7:15
[128] I Corinthians 15

Life Applications of the Holy Spirit

that they are not in control of anything like they assume, so that if your miracle is answered, you will know that it was Jesus who was the One who granted it to you. Then you too will have a testimony and the beginning of a journey of faith, with no more hate. We all start at the same place; no one gets a pass on this, unless we have learned early as children, and taught from the very beginning...[129]

Jesus said "But if I do the miracles, and you don't believe me, believe the works; that you may know and believe that the Father is in me, and I in the Father."[130] ...How many people you know who are on Face Book right now who spew hate combined with hate mongering, and they don't see it in themselves? Two wrongs don't make a right! Others can see it in them, and it does no good to anyone to rebut them, because they are lost in a world of intellectualism that does not make sense, creating frustration like sinking in quick sand without a life line...so we must all pray for them that they receive a miracle soon. Something deep inside is fueling their hate, keeping them unfulfilled, lonely, distant unable to love, and the perpetual victim of unfairness that is not obvious to them, but obvious to everyone else around them.... Be safe, keep the faith, and learn to live in obedience.[131]

...Think about it.

---

[129] Matthew 17:20
[130] John 10:38
[131] John 14:15

Three vs. Three

Are you letting hate,[132] fear,[133] or anger[134] define who you are today? Most of the people who either live with you, work with you, or know you well, can see who you really are, even though you may not see yourself that way because you can be hiding out in one in of the big three destroyers of your life: hate fear, or anger. These three can steal your joy, and then destroy your life because they always show up in words or the actions of most everything you will say or do, either in private or in public.... Remember that in Jeremiah He says, "I the LORD search the heart and examine the mind, to reward each person according to their conduct, according to what their deeds deserve."[135]

So, for the best life to live, don't let another sunrise nor sunset pass you by in which you living with either hate, fear, or anger. Know that God loves you as He made you; and He will keep chasing you down until you finally submit your life back to Him, and also understand that there is no place you can ever hide which will separate you from His Love, Grace, and Mercy.[136]

...Think about it.

---

[132] I John 4:20
[133] Psalm 23:4, John 14:27
[134] James 1:19, Ecclesiastes 7:9, Ephesians 4:26
[135] Jerimiah 17:10
[136] Romans 8:35

Life Applications of the Holy Spirit

Anger is a Choice

Fear, Hate, and Anger seem to all show up together as a single entity in people's lives. These seem to be inseparable once they get hold of a person and it becomes like they are drowning...God loves us so much He tries to keep us from the unhappiness and emotional drowning this brings us...

The Book of Ephesians teaches us how-to live-in peace with more love, and less hate, fear, and anger. It says, "In your anger do not sin. Do not let the sun go down while you are still angry."[137]

The social ripple effect we all create will always be either love which Jesus first showed us[138] or hate an anger; always, please pass along and show love of Jesus, not hate and anger; love it is the better choice.[139]

...Think about it.

---

[137] Ephesians 4:26
[138] I John 4:19, John 3:16
[139] 2 Timothy 2:24

Brian Smith

Our Plans

Are you making big plans today? I did once, when as a young teenager. I wanted to be an NFL super star. But on October 9, 1971, I was in a hunting accident which changed my life. I was in a hunting accident and shot at point blank range with a 12-gauge shotgun.

It was my fault. I had put my hand on a friend's gun barrel when we were hunting to push it away out (of my path) when the shotgun went off made a direct hit to my leg, leaving a large gaping hole in my body, with my blood and muscle quickly leaving me and sending me into shock....That the moment when I stopping making my own plans independent of God; which I made in the past that had no longevity, and started following the plans of Christ, the One who saved me on that day, and who had better plans for me than I could have ever imagined.

Proverbs says, "We can make our plans, but the LORD determines our steps." [140] And this is now even more true today than ever I believe. ...Are you also making your plans and pushing things out of God's path.

---

[140] Proverb s 16:19

Life Applications of the Holy Spirit

In reflection, if I had stepped about two inches forward, I would have died, or two inches back I would have lost my leg, and also maybe never had children. Or… if I had pushed that gun more slowly, I would be dead in the graveyard, today, and on, and on… and the ramifications could be endless. So, think deeply about your own plans today and see if you are truly in step with your Creator and Savior and what this all means in your future as you seek out "Your will be done", or "God's will be done". Blessings.

...Think about it.

Brian Smith

Slow Down, Stop, & Care

I was living and loving only for myself until something out of the ordinary happened one afternoon in 1987. I was number one person in my own life when I received a phone call from a friend, and a mother, when she said to me, "Jessica, (who had been my neighbor & not her real name) has killed herself; and she would have wanted you to be a pallbearer at her funeral. Would you do this for her and for us? Her funeral is this Saturday." Jessica was seventeen.

She was junior in High school. I was a young doctor of twenty-eight years of age. I thought we were worlds apart in our ambitions, goals, and expectations in life, but maybe not so much maybe in ordinary things. For full years while I was attending graduate school, she would come visit and talk after her school let out and hang out because at her own home she was mostly alone, and not a place a she wanted to stay. Jessica in her own way was constantly reaching out. Once she even ran away from home to try to get away from her unhappy life.

I was very busy with my life in school and especially finishing my education. Her family tracked her down in Colorado after she ran away and then brought back against her will. Unfortunately, I did not see the overt signs of her desperation with any urgency to get involved until it was too late. Jessica was very a wounded person who needed to be loved. She needed some special extra help, and really, now I believe all she needed was someone to slow down, stop and pay some attention to her...

About a year before Jessica killed herself, her mother called me and wanted me to meet with Jessica. I explained I have moved pretty far away, that I was a doctor, and now we lived more than a

Life Applications of the Holy Spirit

hundred of miles apart, so I thought it would be best if she found someone her own age to be in her life as her friend. Now, I regret not taking just a bit of my precious time, to stop and help an injured person in need. But I did not understand then, what I understand now as I understand after reading the parable of the Good Samaritan in Luke Chapter 10.

Here is what is says... Jesus spoke saying, "'Love the Lord your God with all your heart and with all your soul and with all your strength and with all your mind; and, 'Love your neighbor as yourself. Do this and you will live. "But there was ONE WHO WANTED TO JUSTIFY HIMSELF, so he asked Jesus, "And who is my neighbor?"[141]

This is the same question which each gets asked each of us over and over again in our public and in our private lives, internally and externally, morally and immorally, financially and non-financially, spiritually and non-spiritually, racially and non-racially, sexually and non-sexually, victimized or non-victimized, rich and poor, happy and sad, free and slave...but how many of us avoid wanting to face the question dead on?

All of us in this life will not find peace until we can answer this question as it pertains to our legacy; and, then do the right thing, not by our own understanding but of the understanding that supersedes our own from up above.... So, again the question is asked one more time: "Who is your neighbor?"[142] And what is Jesus asking you to do about it?

...Think about it.

---

[141] Luke 10:25-37
[142] John 10: 27-37

Brian Smith

Be Humble

Have you ever been traveling in a car, you know the driver, and they are obviously lost, and they continue to be lost because their pride won't let them stop to ask directions? Then, out of dead silence (because no one is talking) someone from the back seat or maybe the front seat says kindly, "hey dad (or mom) why don't you just stop and ask for directions so we can all get there on time?" Or maybe, "Honey, I think we might want to stop and ask someone where the place is. How does that sound?", or maybe, "We are going to be late and we might miss the party if we don't stop and get directions." Do these questions seem hurtful or helpful to you?

The comments are not gender specific, nor meant to be negative in any way, just helpful to all traveling together. But they can be interpreted as humiliating in insecure relationships. The same goes for spiritual relationships. The heart leads the person who is driving, and leading the group and not the mind. When the heart is hardened by pride the person driving will not stop, humble themselves and acknowledge that are lost, and that they need help. Life in general is allot like this!

Life Applications of the Holy Spirit

The Bible the Book of Proverbs says this about pride, "With pride comes only contention, but wisdom is with the well-advised. Pride only breeds quarrels, but with ones who take advice is wisdom. An evil man in disgrace does evil, and those who are counseled are wise. Arrogance produces only quarreling, but those who take advice gain wisdom."[143]

...Think about it.

---

[143] Proverbs 13:10

Brian Smith

Hardened Heart

Who or what could a free person possibly be mad at and in rebellion with today? Could perhaps they be mad or rebelling against their own selves? Or God? Or a neighbor? Or a member of their own family? Maybe poor health? Or bad judgement? Perhaps it is with past actions. Or past voices? Is it perhaps with a bleak future? Don't you think they can see it and just say it out loud and acknowledge it!

What is it that is causing so many to be unhappy and makes us so angry? It is easy. We want to be God, and we are not Gog. We have only two choices in life with two distinct paths to choose from, only two. A few strong souls with a heart for serving will follow the first choice: following in the footsteps of Christ and learn how to forgive and to live in peace and harmony with the blessings of self-control. The other choice is to become distracted, and think we are just as good as God. We soon become unfocused, selfish, egotistical, prideful, lonely, lack of self-control and hardened over time from unmet expectations regarding love, hope, joy, and friendship acting like we are God and become unhappy we cannot control things we thought we could..

The Book of Psalm teaches us how to reflect and pray if we need to be rescued from a personal rebellion and a hardened heart...

"Lord, remind me how brief my time on earth will be.
Remind me that my days are numbered—
how fleeting my life is.
You have made my life no longer than the width of my hand.
My entire lifetime is just a moment to you;
at best, each of us is but a breath."
We are merely moving shadows,

Life Applications of the Holy Spirit

and all our busy rushing ends in nothing.
We heap up wealth,
not knowing who will spend it.
And so, Lord, where do I put my hope?
My only hope is in you!
Rescue me from my rebellion.
Do not let fools mock me.
I am silent before you; I won't say a word,
for my punishment is from you.
But please stop striking me!
I am exhausted by the blows from your hand.
When you discipline us for our sins,
you consume like a moth what is precious to us.
Each of us is but a breath.
Hear my prayer, O Lord!
Listen to my cries for help!
Don't ignore my tears.
For I am your guest—
a traveler passing through,
as my ancestors were before me.[144]

So, we all pray Lord, please rescue us... that we might live and abide in your grace and peace, receiving the blessings of Your Love and Your continued Mercy forever; as we rebel no more, totally giving our rebellions over to you and leaving them at your feet...whatever they might be.[145]

...Think about it!

---

[144] Psalm 39:4-13
[145] I Samuel 15:23, Proverbs 17:11

Brian Smith

Color of the Heart

Have you researched and published one or more books regarding on the subject of race in America as a topic of "Man" vs. "Mankind"?[146] I have and I have addressed straight on in my book "Johnnie Spot Perfect". It is the second book of my series "Thy Kingdom Come", and it can be ordered along-side the rest of the series at my website www.drbriansmithbooks.com.

In the series I explain how God has created each person perfect in his or her own skin by virtue of the person's gifts and talents. Every creation is created different, even within the same culture and color of skin. The Creator is not so much concerned with the color of the skin he gave each, or the situation in which He placed them, but He is more concerned about the color of their heart which they develop and choose to follow. The Holy Spirit watches closely to see if a person's heart becomes hardened in the process and see if it becomes rebellious against His will. And therein lies the measure of a person's merits or not for Him.

Fear, hate, and anger always get in our way of having a heart that is open to Him. These are the main weapons which Satan uses to control us and move us away from the love we long for and blessings which are reserved for us. The three emotions ultimately cause us to sin in our hearts and then fall from grace in our lives because we will not lean on God's promise of salvation in true hope.[147]

If race becomes an issue to anyone, then he or she must choose and search in then their heart for that which a person judges… that

---

[146] I Corinthians 10:13, Galatians 5:13
[147] Galatians 5

Life Applications of the Holy Spirit

he or she will be similarly judged against them.[148] For race will not be an item of delineation in Heaven, so why is it here on earth? There will only be one race, and that will be the race of the children of The Lord. If it was not true, then Heaven would be no different than it is here today, and we are promised that it is not.[149]

    ...Think about it.

---

[148] Matthew 7:1
[149] John 11:40

Brian Smith

The Orchestra

Have you ever tried listening to an orchestra when all the player's instruments are not all-in tune? Even as the whole system of fine musicians tune their different instruments which they hold close to them, they produce a horrid non-melodious cacophony of noise they produce until they all are tuned one by one individually and then they play together in sync. I believe that God looks down upon His creation sometimes and listens to the harmony (or disharmony) produced by His symphony of players. This symphony or orchestra might be well within the walls of a local church, or within a family, or a school, or a business, or even much larger as a society. When the players are not in tune with each other and the maestro, then the music is not music, it is just noise.

And if a musician (like one of God's team) says to another: I am better than you...or my instrument is more in tune, so you should follow my lead, then the maestro cannot have music made in sync for others to hear. Peter said it best with these words, "Finally, all of you, live in harmony with one another, be sympathetic, love as brothers, be compassionate and humble."[150] There can only be one maestro who resides in Heaven, and only He can lead the beautiful song or music. It is never the players.... or it is just noise.

...Think about it.

---

[150] I Peter 3:8

Life Applications of the Holy Spirit

Five Star Rating

Routinely we rate one another in the world today based on a made-up, irrelevant and quite ambiguous 5-star rating system derived was from some mind of some obscure individual used on the internet to control groups for power and wealth. The nebulous rating system uses no facts… only emotional feelings.

This 5-start subjective rating system can become personal, because ultimately it is "all about me vs. you". And the system can be weaponized often used to destroy rather than build up as other systems are meant to do.

All subjective rating systems are morally corrupt. They soon become a standard in a world of self-centered ideology that reeks of foul odors resulting in foolish behaviors giving biased opinions on things not worthy of being rated.

So, subjectiveness is the truly a fault ridden system of the blind leading the blind.[151] Just look and see how much underserving merit is soon divided between different masses where therein their personal freedom, common sense, high moral standards all combined with precious liberty are divided and contained. Please run, hide and ask for forgiveness if you have drunk this candy-flavored addicting cool-aid.

If you like being subjective in your judgement of others, and not objective, have you ever thought is asked just how many stars God might give you, if God only rating you based on His feelings?[152]

---

[151] Matthew 15:14
[152] John 8:7-8

Brian Smith

I will suggest using this 5-star rating system if you want to judge other people. 1.) Jesus said to His followers, "If you had faith, even as small as a mustard seed, you could say to this mountain, 'Move from here to there,' and it would move. Nothing would be impossible."[153] =1 star... 2.) Then Jesus said with faith know that, "What good is it, dear brothers and sisters, if you say you have faith but don't show it by your actions? Can that kind of faith save anyone?"[154] =1 star.... 3.) Followed Jesus asking for public acknowledgment saying, "Everyone who acknowledges me publicly here on earth, I will also acknowledge before my Father in heaven."[155] =1 start....4.) and then how do measure up living responsibly with others? To them who followed and learned from Him: "The master said, 'Well done, my good and faithful servant. You have been faithful in handling this small amount, so now I will give you many more responsibilities. Let's celebrate together!'[156] =1 star... 5.) and then to John, the one chosen to follow Him that He loved most, He said... "There is no greater love than to lay down one's life for one's friends.[157] =1 star.

This makes a 1+1+1+1+1= a 5-Star heavenly rating system would be a good starting point for us to use as a matter of discussion if God were the one grading each of us today based on if we are attentive or not to The Holy Spirit's counsel and leading. One day He will actually do our grading of how we lived.... What will be your score? & How did you think you will do? Blessings.

...Think about it.

---

[153] Matthew 17:10
[154] James 2: 14-26
[155] Matthew 10:32-33
[156] Matthew 15:23
[157] John 15:13

Life Applications of the Holy Spirit

The Racist

I was sitting with a group of friends recently when the topic of "Racism" surfaced... So, I asked each of them if they would please define what the word "Racism" meant to them? and what being a "racist" really means in everyday terminology?

Each of them shared their definition of "racism" from a personal view point. It seems none of their definitions agreed. And we as a nation cannot agree on a definition anymore because we each refuse to be taught from any higher authority. Basically, we are a nation of arrogant fools. It seems that everyone just wants their own opinion herd while silencing others and this leads to chaos, anger, bitterness and ultimately division, divisiveness, angst and turmoil.

This corrupt disharmony leads to an altered state of personal praise, worship, and secular insanity which then becomes the classic example of the blind leading the blind without proper instruction or correction, and waiting on their leader to come to lead them. In history, this is called a "Golden Calf or Sin of the Calf" moment in time.[158]

To help enlighten the group, I followed up with this second question, "Ok, so does being a racist mean being "For-a-Group" of specific people or Against-a-Group" of specific people?... Which is it? Because both statements are being said and each are equally disconcerting?" Every uneducated fool will choose one side or the other, showing total ignorance in their judgement while making a choice of the hill they wish to die upon.[159]

---

[158] Exodus 32:4
[159] John 8:7

It is a human tendency that when personal safety becomes an issue, to-become-against God's righteousness which is the best social posture or social punitive actions will occur. Then the ugly head the of bigotry, prejudice, and discrimination ensue. Jesus in His own words, taught us not to judge by Man's values when He said in the Book of Matthew "Why do you look at the speck of sawdust in your brother's eye and pay no attention to the plank in your own eye? How can you say to your brother, 'Let me take the speck out of your eye,' when all the time there is a plank in your own eye? You hypocrite, first take the plank out of your own eye, and then you will see clearly to remove the speck from your brother's eye."[160]

This was that way it was two and five millennia ago while not much has changed today when we try to live without God's teachings or His values.

...Think about it.

---

[160] Matthew 7:3-5

Life Applications of the Holy Spirit

The Mountain

Has God given you a certain mountain to climb? Or have you chosen your own specific mountain to surpass? Eventually, everyone will need counsel from the Holy Spirit, as Christ's Advocate, to find your way over their mountain.

Within the past two days I received three messages.

1.) One of my life-life friends is very close to losing their battle with throat cancer

2.) One of my friends just lost their mom this week.

3.) One of my friends lost two wonderful nieces in a car accident. The two were girls were just ages 14 and 16. Each of these families have been given a mountain of sorrow to climb.

Where would our lives look like if we had little or no hope in any rewards in the after-life?

In an unprecedented Biblical event, Jesus took several of His disciples onto a mountain where He showed them his transfiguration from immaculate conception back to the spiritually incarnate as He passed over and spoke with souls who had passed over before Him. It was there that Jesus allowed Mankind to witness the immortality of Eternal Life.[161]

God gave Moses the "Ten Commandments" on Mount Sinai[162] while in the Book of Revelation an angel of God carried John in the

---

[161] Matthew 17:2
[162] Exodus 34

Spirit to a mountain, great and high, and showed him the Holy City, Jerusalem, coming down out of heaven from God.[163]

If you or someone you know are on a mountain climbing hard, in the Book of John, Jesus said to those who followed Him... "Anyone who loves me will obey my teaching. My Father will love them, and we will come to them and make our home with them. Anyone who does not love me will not obey my teaching. These words you hear are not my own; they belong to the Father who sent me. "All this I have spoken while still with you. But the Advocate, the Holy Spirit, whom the Father will send in my name, will teach you all things and will remind you of everything I have said to you. Peace I leave with you; my peace I give you. I do not give to you as the world gives. Do not let your hearts be troubled and do not be afraid."

There is no need to spend more time climbing personal mountains that don't matter in the kingdom of God. Give your mountain a rest and deliver yourself to wholly to Christ who wants to take all mountains away so that you will receive counsel from the Holy Spirit and get peace. Fear not, and do not tarry. Come off the mountain and begin to enjoy the lush meadows and fertile valleys that have been waiting for you.

...Think about it.

---

[163] John 14:24-27

Life Applications of the Holy Spirit

The Truth

How much of all man's conflict, anger, hatred, fear, and vengeance today is because of what is taught wrongly from father to son? Maybe this stem from having not having a Father at all, or limited to having a limited father??? Or perhaps a demonic force has been creating circles of misinformation around you, telling you lies, making distractions in relationships, or establishing bad examples of truth and love towards you or them? If these things encompass you surround you or someone you know, then you or they are lost, and have been listening to and applying the principle of self-annihilation.

This conflict cycle goes on and on from one day to night, and one problem to the next until the problem is recognized, acknowledged and snuffed out... Until the sin will control people actions and their behavior. When will the world and its people recognize the Truth, and the one and only Truth will set them free?[164]

For thousands of years, the world has not moved away from untruth on any large scale.... Empires come and go, victims are created in the name of goodness and then multiplied ad infinitum, and the sin of the world just keeps popping like growing mounds of popcorn in a huge cooking kettle, looking for one more human to lead the world to redemption, but it seldom happens.

Go ahead and seek out the grave of any famous person other than Jesus Christ who ruled the world for more and a few years and you will find no immortal statues, no long lines line weeping over graves, and no markers that endure the test of time because with time

---

[164] John 8:32

all names in history are lost among the sin of the world. One and only "The One" who could not be kept in the grave, is the one name, "Jesus Christ" who name still endures after two thousand years as the Savior-To- The-World. It is good for everyone to reflect, read, and remember what Jesus said in the Book of John 8 when He spoke to the people of the time who were 25-40% slaves in the Roman Empire....

To the Jews who had believed him, Jesus said, "If you hold to my teaching, you are really my disciples. Then you will know the truth, and the truth will set you free."

They answered him, "We are Abraham's descendants and have never been slaves of anyone. How can you say that we shall be set free?"

Jesus replied, "Very truly I tell you, everyone who sins is a slave to sin. Now a slave has no permanent place in the family, but a son belongs to it forever. So if the Son sets you free, you will be free indeed. I know that you are Abraham's descendants. Yet you are looking for a way to kill me, because you have no room for my word. I am telling you what I have seen in the Father's presence, and you are doing what you have heard from your father."

"Abraham is our father," they replied.

"If you were Abraham's children," said Jesus, "then you would do what Abraham did. As it is, you are looking for a way to kill me, a man who has told you the truth that I heard from God. Abraham did not do such things. You are doing the works of your own father."

"We are not illegitimate children," they protested. "The only Father we have is God himself."

Jesus said to them, "If God were your Father, you would love me, for I have come here from God. I have not come on my own; God sent me. Why is my language not clear to you? Because you are unable to hear what I say. You belong to your father, the devil, and you want to carry out your father's desires. He was a murderer from the beginning, not holding to the truth, for there is no truth in him. When he lies, he speaks his native language, for he is a liar and

Life Applications of the Holy Spirit

the father of lies. Yet because I tell the truth, you do not believe me! Can any of you prove me guilty of sin? If I am telling the truth, why don't you believe me? Whoever belongs to God hears what God says. The reason you do not hear is that you do not belong to God."

The Jews answered him, "Aren't we right in saying that you are a Samaritan and demon-possessed?"

"I am not possessed by a demon," said Jesus, "but I honor my Father and you dishonor me. I am not seeking glory for myself; but there is one who seeks it, and he is the judge. Very truly I tell you, whoever obeys my word will never see death."

At this they exclaimed, "Now we know that you are demon-possessed! Abraham died and so did the prophets, yet you say that whoever obeys your word will never taste death. Are you greater than our father Abraham? He died, and so did the prophets. Who do you think you are?"

Jesus replied, "If I glorify myself, my glory means nothing. My Father, whom you claim as your God, is the one who glorifies me. Though you do not know him, I know him. If I said I did not, I would be a liar like you, but I do know him and obey his word. Your father Abraham rejoiced at the thought of seeing my day; he saw it and was glad."

"You are not yet fifty years old," they said to him, "and you have seen Abraham!"
"Very truly I tell you," Jesus answered, "before Abraham was born, I am!" At this, they picked up stones to stone him, but Jesus hid himself, slipping away from the temple grounds.[165]

Believe in the Truth, and the Truth will set you free, for the Great I Am has told you it is so...

...Think about it.

---

[165] John 8:33-59

Brian Smith

Coveting

What is one of the most unused and least talked about words in the English language? I believe it is the word "covet". This word is the root of most of the unhappiness in our world today, and it is a disease of the heart... It means to yearn for something that someone else has which it is not yours. It is also the 9th Commandment, which says, "Thou shalt not covet". [166]

When is the last time you heard this word used outside of church? Probably never… because I have not either. Today is a Sunday and a good time to perhaps get up and go to church and listen about God's laws on successful living and what to do about coveting.

You will never hear about not to covet on secular television, secular music, secular entertainment, secular purchasing, secular voting, or secular education or by a self-serving world who exploits its personal messages to gain wealth or power; in fact, the worldly message is just the opposite!

So, what will a man or woman covet that they are willing to beg, borrow, or steal for? Perhaps even covet to act as a proxy, or act as an agitator or be and activist for and then not even know what they are doing it for? Could it be that maybe you mentally might just covet another's wife, or another's husband, or another's riches or status, another's home or another's family? Do you as an individual covert the need for more security, happiness, love, fulfillment, food, sleep, freedom, liberty, ease, service, entertainment, health,

---

[166] Exodus 20:17

Life Applications of the Holy Spirit

protection, family ties, etc....? None of these are guaranteed in life without Jesus; and none if any are deserved for what other reason?

No-one gets to choose the time nor place in which they were born, nor the family in which they have been born into, nor the color of their skin they adorn, nor the location of their birth, nor the circumstances of their health, nor the wealth of their family, and so on, and so on....

But, if you think any of these are something to be fretted over or to worry over because your life and living has been unfair to you, then you ultimately will end up becoming bitter, and being lost and then become a heathen, a dark angel, or a pagan by simple character definition, and then losing your own heart to being less than its original design requiring post-mortem adjudication.

So, what is it that one might covet that belongs to someone else without bad effects? Nothing! Coveting is an addiction, a disease, that is much worse and harder to cure than immoral sex, dependency on drugs or alcohol, gambling, or unfaithfulness because coveting has eternal consequences just the same, and so tied and bound with the others? Without Jesus a person will always covet something and always be without peace in their heart. Truly accept Christ as the Savior, and you will be cured of the disease and you will covet no more.[167]

...Think about it.

---

[167] Romans 10:9-10

Brian Smith

God's Opinion

Have you ever heard the saying, "Am I my brother's keeper"? It comes from the first part of the Bible regarding the first two sons of Adam and Eve… after the fall. Cain, was the older brother, and Abel, was the younger brother. Both boys gave sacrifices to God but, Abel's gained more favor. This resulted in the first case of hate, fear, anger, and jealously causing a crime. Cain in his sin murders his younger brother; who had gained more favor in God's eyes. God was watching them closely, and knew what had happened. So, after the crime, God asks Cain to see if his heart is repentant and will take responsibility for his actions, but instead Cain answers with a hardened heart, and with a lie, trying to spin the Truth saying, "I don't know, am I my brother's keeper?" For his punishment God banishes Cain, and sends him away.[168]

When God asks each of us after some-thing sinful we have done which is not as He would approve, how do we answer Him?... With irresponsibly and a spin just like Cain? And with that do we get one step closer from being banished from Heaven?

We know that Heaven is not run like a democracy. And so much of the way we think about the correctness of our actions today, will not apply in God's Kingdom. Only God's opinion matters and only God's opinion counts.

So, we will either ask for forgiveness and seek out mercy, or we will lie, trying to spin the truth, and take no responsibility for our actions, resulting in being totally separated from Him. So, it seems

---

[168] Genesis 4:1-13

Life Applications of the Holy Spirit

that not much has changed since the "First Family of Mankind" in history was recorded several thousands of years ago.

    We must remember that God is always watching us, and if we sin, as we all do, it is better to repent and ask for forgiveness than to lie and not take responsibility for our actions resulting in being separated from God for eternity.

    …Think about it.

Brian Smith

Who Are You?

Have you ever attended an event, when a stranger walks up to you and asks this direct question, "Who are you?" The most common response given is to answer with something (or someone) we associate with and maybe we also love. Women usually will answer something related to a relationship like, "I am Stacy's daughter, or Lisa's sister, Johnnie's mother, Bob's wife, Granny's step daughter," and so on... Men usually answer something related to their work like, " I am a home inspector, a lawyer, a dentist, I work at XYZ company in finance, or I am just a nobody looking for a place to sit down and rest," etc... the answer a person gives often says more about that person than we think.

In each of their ways, our answer is usually reflective on future security as related to what we love. But our lives are all temporal; and everything we have that we love may come to an end quicker on earth here than we think. For a good long healthy life, we humans may live approximately 35,000 days. How many days do you think you have left? Maybe just one, who knows but God Himself?

Jesus said in His own words in the Book of Matthew: "If you love your father or mother more than you love me, you are not worthy of being mine; or if you love your son or daughter more than me, you are not worthy of being mine. If you refuse to take up your cross and follow me, you are not worthy of being mine. If you cling to your life, you will lose it; but if you give up your life for me, you will find it."[169]

---

[169] Matthew 10:37-39

Life Applications of the Holy Spirit

So, just maybe when we all die, and we all cross over from this life to the next, Jesus or someone else assigned to adjudicate our lives may be there waiting for us and they may also ask us the same question, "So, who are you?"

It is my prayer that each of us will answer correctly before our Creator by associating with Him who we love; rather than how we answer this question at an event. How you will answer the question the next time you are asked by a stranger?... because Jesus will know if you have associated with the world and not Him, and refused to take up your cross and not followed Him.[170] Or, if you have chosen to follow Him with your complete heart, body, and soul. By your words He will know you and you will be justified or acquitted.[171]

For myself, I will hopefully be given the opportunity to answer one day, "It is I, your faithful and loving servant."[172] And I hope you also do too...

...Think about it.

---

[170] Matthew 10:33
[171] Matthew 12:37
[172] John 14:15

Brian Smith

Hate

I looked up in the Bible to see what it says about "hate" since this topic seems to be ubiquitous when it comes to strident conversation; and also, what does "God hate" if He does actually hate?

The topic of "Hate" is addressed 127 times in the Bible… 91 times in the Old Testament and 36 times in the New Testament. I believe it is important to for us to seek out this information, understand it's true meaning, and reflect upon what the Bible says what "God hates", and then do our best to not participate what He does not like.

Here is what the Bible says, "There are six things the Lord hates…seven that are detestable to him: haughty eyes, a lying tongue, hands that shed innocent blood, a heart that devises wicked schemes, feet that are quick to rush into evil, a false witness who pours out lies, and a person who stirs up conflict in the community." [173]

These actions should be permanently established in our brains as focal reminders of what not to do, try to avoid, and also in quiet time to think and pray about. God is watching us all the time, and in the end, it is only His opinion and judgement that really counts.

…Think about it.

---

[173] Proverbs 6:16-19

Life Applications of the Holy Spirit

The Definition

If you say you are a "Believer", what does this mean? The word "believe" is derived from two-word parts which means "By-Life", and translating to what you believe-in will show up in your-life. Then other people can see what you believe in and it will show up in your life. For instance: how you spend your money, how you raise up your children, how you deal with stress, or how you deal with relationships, etc...

In the Book of 2 Corinthians, the scripture explains how to keep what a person believes in protected and true, "Be ye not unequally yoked together with unbelievers: for what fellowship hath righteousness with unrighteousness? and what communion hath light with darkness?"[174]

This is a message of "prevention" (not action) to God's people whom He loves. God does not want anyone to live a life of misery, but many of us do. The scripture is painting a picture for us explaining to us that a yoke is very similar to a "wooden cross" where two animals are bound together to "be a team" to do specific work, and that is pull a load resulting the best fruits of labor for its Master.

But what is the result of a yoke when one animal or people is pulling one way and the other animal or person is pulling the other way? The two will work against each other and the load becomes much hard to pull. One individual (or animal) is trying to over-power the other, and the work gets quite tiring, and no fruit will be made

---

[174] 2 Corinthians 6:14

for a Master when two incompatible beasts or people are to become yoked.

The yoke can be either two people in marriage, or it can be a single person at work, or it can be an institution where the yoke can be government decrees placed its people, etc... Whatever the "Yoke" is, you will see it in the "Life" of the person, or a people as they struggle to perform even the simplest of duties and decisions. Being yoked, is an exercise in submission and kindness, and if God has placed the yoke, only He can remove it.[175] It gets mighty tiring trying to fight something or someone, or some cause which you may be yoked with. The real question is, how will your life's legacy show to others what "you really believe" .... And why is our world in so much pain, strife, and personal duress?

...Think about it.

---

[175] Galatians 5:13

Life Applications of the Holy Spirit

Lazy Servant

Do you know the difference between being a "Disciple" and being an "Apostle" of Christ? A "disciple" is a student of a teacher (which is good), and an apostle is a missionary, messenger, and traveler (which is harder but better). Both are servants, but how much effort do they work for their Master?

The first twelve men whom Jesus recruited and taught, were his original twelve disciples, but after Jesus went away to Heaven, He left them behind to be His missionaries, (The Twelve Apostles) of His message. Paul was converted after Jesus' death to also become the Apostle/Missionary to the Gentiles.

For the twelve original disciples, Jesus taught them His parables about what being good students and servants looked like; and what all nations should look like when the word has been spread to the world. History recounts that America was founded fundamentally on basic taught Christian principles upon the Judaean-Christian Laws and has received much wealth since inception. Question: Has America sent out enough messengers to spread the gospel of Jesus to continue please God ad infinitum??? Could it be possible, that God be sending the rest of the world as immigrants to America to hear the message of Christ instead?... Because they need to hear it? Jesus said, "What good is it if a man gain's the whole world and loses his soul?"[176] And for a family or person to move from one pagan environment to another and receive only gold and wealth (or milk and honey) only, and not receive the Gospel of Christ is to remain lost without Christ throughout eternity... Listen to Jesus' Parable of the Bags of Gold in the Book of Matthew:

---

[176] Mark 8:36

14 "Again, it will be like a man going on a journey, who called his servants and entrusted his wealth to them. 15 To one he gave five bags of gold, to another two bags, and to another one bag, each according to his ability. Then he went on his journey. 16 The man who had received five bags of gold went at once and put his money to work and gained five bags more. 17 So also, the one with two bags of gold gained two more. 18 But the man who had received one bag went off, dug a hole in the ground and hid his master's money.

19 "After a long time the master of those servants returned and settled accounts with them. 20 The man who had received five bags of gold brought the other five. 'Master,' he said, 'you entrusted me with five bags of gold. See, I have gained five more.'

21 "His master replied, 'Well done, good and faithful servant! You have been faithful with a few things; I will put you in charge of many things. Come and share your master's happiness!'

22 "The man with two bags of gold also came. 'Master,' he said, 'you entrusted me with two bags of gold; see, I have gained two more.'

23 "His master replied, 'Well done, good and faithful servant! You have been faithful with a few things; I will put you in charge of many things. Come and share your master's happiness!'

24 "Then the man who had received one bag of gold came. 'Master,' he said, 'I knew that you are a hard man, harvesting where you have not sown and gathering where you have not scattered seed. 25 So I was afraid and went out and hid your gold in the ground. See, here is what belongs to you.'

26 "His master replied, 'You wicked, lazy servant! So, you knew that I harvest where I have not sown and gather where I have not scattered seed? 27 Well then, you should have put my money on deposit with the bankers, so that when I returned, I would have received it back with interest.

Life Applications of the Holy Spirit

28 "'So take the bag of gold from him and give it to the one who has ten bags. 29 For whoever has will be given more, and they will have an abundance. Whoever does not have, even what they have will be taken from them. 30 And throw that worthless servant outside, into the darkness, where there will be weeping and gnashing of teeth.'[177]... So, now,...

...Think about it.

---

[177] Matthew 25:14-30

Brian Smith

Distracted Christians

The older I get, the more I dig deep into Jesus' words to search for my own life for answers. Since I was a child, the parable of the ten virgins [178] with their lamps and their lamp oil in has always been confusing to me. What did he mean by "virgins", and their "lamps, and lamp oil"? The ending of the Parable was clear: "Will you be ready when He returns", but what was the rest of the meaning? Why didn't He say, "There are ten good people, or ten followers? Are these virgins male or female? Is this a message for just the sexually pure and no-one else?

My thoughts today are that this message is for the reborn in Christ; not the unbelievers, the pagans, and ungodly. It is for those who have without pressure chosen Him, and have chosen to live and follow His commandments as he asked. It is for those who are now clean from vices and are virgins to acts of cheating, lying, having false Gods, murder (including unborn children) bearing false witness, etc.... as well as pornography, adultery, and other sexually impure thoughts and activities. Jesus always wanted His followers to hold the highest standards: love your enemy, turn your cheek, carry your cross, etc... These are very high standards for sure and not an easy walk ever, especially with the fear of being fed to lions, nailed to a tree, or whipped and beaten for your faith. Christians today are soft and too often distracted from the work that needs to be done.

---

[178] Matthew 25

Life Applications of the Holy Spirit

In the parable, those who are virgins (reborn believers) will have lives (lamps) whose oil (morals, faith, walk, etc...) will be their fuel which will be their legacy. If Jesus came tonight at midnight... how many of the reborn Christians will be wise to have the fuel ready to be accepted; and how many reborn Christians will want to go out and quickly refuel with some form of Holy sanctification, but there will not be enough time. Jesus has said several times, He will not know many of those who say Lord, Lord, and do things in His name.[179] And in this parable, the door gets closed even to the virgin(s) who are pure when he arrives.

...Think about it.

---

[179] Matthew 7:21

Brian Smith

Why Go to a Church?

Who can answer this question, "Am I a giver" or "Am I a taker" honestly? ... Most everyone is living dual personalities with one personality for others around them and the other personality for themselves. This is nothing more than non-transparency unable to answer the hard questions in life truthfully. But there is another question that always leads to the answer to this question!

I had an honest discussion recently with a friend who does not go to church...so I asked them why? They said that they were brought up in a family that went to church on Sundays, but they did not like "having to go" so he stopped when they moved out of the house. When I asked him why not try going again, they said because they did not ever get anything out of going so it was a waste of time.

And when I asked another question, if had he tried going to a different church or denomination to compare churches, and he repeated same the same thing: "I did not receive anything from going to church". Well, I will to admit I had somewhat the same experience until I got a little more mature. I prayed about it one day when I did not feel like going, and the Holy Spirit enlightened me of a small truth that I was missing... It was that attending church was not what I should receive from going, but rather what I needed to give to it by going. This completely changed my attitude about attending church.

Some people may not agree this, but for me, this changed my whole reason for going to church. I was no longer going to be taker; I was going to be a giver! No longer was I experience it like going to the movies, to be entertained, or like attending a musical concerto get inspired, or to get a feel-good message that would last me one

Life Applications of the Holy Spirit

week until I needed another fix, or just feel better about myself for attending and taking it off of my check-off list.

I completely understood that church now was not about being a taker sitting or standing as the music and sermon were read, but being a giver where and when my help was needed. Life is allot like that too.

People who attend church (or perhaps synagogue) as roaming travelers, are always takers because they have missed the reason for attending. Those who move from one location to another, are never satisfied with the message or the church body, nor will they ever be because they are going for the wrong reasons...But the "House of the Lord" is really not a place anyway, is it? Church is a group of people who choose to join themselves in a community and church family to give to each other whole heartily as the body of the church.[180]

It is my contention that if a person is not faithfully and giving to the body of Christ, in some form or fashion and in all things which they own with a joyful attitude of giving[181]...then that person not a true giver of the heart, and they are a taker.

In other words, being a Christian means acting a verb, and not a noun. It means being in action and using hands and feet with the skills and gifts which God have given freely,[182] and not handing out destructive opinions or unruly things when they are not called for[183]...

---

[180] Acts 20:28
[181] Ephesians 4:1-32
[182] Matthew 10:8
[183] I Corinthians 12

Admirable Christian traits are giving, serving, smiling, caring, praying, tithing, waving, parking cars, cleaning floors, putting up chairs, teaching, changing diapers, dusting, making coffee, hosting events, opening your home, sharing problems, visiting hospital, feeding the sick, fostering children, working at orphanages, raising money for homeless, and helping little old ladies cross the street, etc...for then you will investing in your future in Heaven, and in your neighbor; not things that can rust, tarnish, or be stolen from you in the night.[184]

...Think about it.

---

[184] Matthew 6:19-20

Life Applications of the Holy Spirit

The Parable of the Sower

When Sunday arrives in a few days, will you listen with an open heart to a pastor's message either in person or online? And if you do, how soft and fertile will be your heart be to receive a special message delivered which you may by just for you... Our Lord, Jesus of Nazareth, spoke and taught in symbolism many times so that His listeners could relate and perhaps project themselves into the message; but not all could relate, as it is the same today...Listen to Jesus' words in His message to those listening around Him about two thousand years ago on The Parable of the Sower:[185]

That day Jesus went out of the house and sat by the lake. Such large crowds gathered around him that he got into a boat and sat in it, while all the people stood on the shore. Then he told them many things in parables, saying: "A farmer went out to sow his seed. As he was scattering the seed, some fell along the path, and the birds came and ate it up. Some fell on rocky places, where it did not have much soil. It sprang up quickly, because the soil was shallow. But when the sun came up, the plants were scorched, and they withered because they had no root. Other seed fell among thorns, which grew up and choked the plants. Still other seed fell on good soil, where it produced a crop—a hundred, sixty or thirty times what was sown. Whoever has ears, let them hear."

The disciples came to him and asked, "Why do you speak to the people in parables?"

He replied, "Because the knowledge of the secrets of the kingdom of heaven has been given to you, but not to them. Whoever

---

[185] Matthew 13:1-18

has will be given more, and they will have an abundance. Whoever does not have, even what they have will be taken from them. This is why I speak to them in parables:

"Though seeing, they do not see;
though hearing, they do not hear or understand.
 In them is fulfilled the prophecy of Isaiah:
"'You will be ever hearing but never understanding;
you will be ever seeing but never perceiving.
For this people's heart has become calloused;
they hardly hear with their ears,
and they have closed their eyes.
Otherwise, they might see with their eyes,
hear with their ears,
understand with their hearts
and turn, and I would heal them.

But blessed are your eyes because they see, and your ears because they hear. For truly I tell you, many prophets and righteous people longed to see what you see but did not see it, and to hear what you hear but did not hear it."

...Think about it.

Life Applications of the Holy Spirit

Slave vs. No-Slave

WHO IS THE MOST FAMOUS SLAVE OF ALL TIME?
What color of shin did he have? "Where was he from?" And how did his life end?" "What was his life like and what was his lot?"

Historians have written much and immortalized a man called Spartacus who was a captured and turned into a white slave. He was born in Thrace in the year 111BC. He was captured by the Roman army, and then turned into a slave Gladiator to fight for entertainment and sport...He escaped then after, leading a slave revolt with tens of thousands of other white slaves who followed him, he threatened the Roman Empire, then he was captured and with 6,000 slaves of those who followed him. When finally defeated, the survivors were each crucified along the Appian Way for participating in the revolt against the empire which was before the coming of Christ in 71BC, over two millennia ago.

Spartacus's legacy has out-lasted many other famous slave gladiators like Crixus (probably from France), Gannicus (most likely from Germany), Castus (maybe Switzerland or Luxembourg), and Oenomaus (also probably from France); but all these are rarely taught about or referred to in the history of world slavery because they are not representative of the times in which we live.

Another famous slave of historical notoriety is Joseph,[186] who was captured and sold into slavery by his brothers into Egypt for 20 pieces of silver as historically referenced important in the Book of Genesis.

---

[186] Genesis 37:28

And there was also Saul, (another good choice for most famous slave), who was knocked down from off his horse on his way to Damascus in the historical recorded of Acts 9, when the ascended Lord after his resurrection said to him, "Saul, Saul, why do you persecute me? I am Jesus whom you are persecuting." Saul was called to become an Apostle to the Gentiles and preach the Gospel to all who were before him, and I believe He became the most famous slave of all time in our history books....as you read his words to the Romans in the Book of Romans (note the definition between slavery and being a servant can be subtle; slavery usually ends in death as the understood way out, being a servant does not).

Paul did not meet Jesus when Jesus was in his incarnated human body, but only after Jesus' death and His resurrection in a new spiritual body did Paul see Him, just like those who follow Him today and have met with Him only after the resurrection. Afterwards, the Apostle Paul went on a personal mission to spread the Gospel of Christ's message until his death. Paul voluntarily marched into Rome to meet with Emperor Nero face to face to deliver the message of the good news of Christ to the most powerful man on the planet. Paul was shortly thereafter beheaded on the Ostian Way (as a captive of the Roman Empire and as a slave of His Lord Jesus Christ) between 64 and 67AD.

The Apostle Paul wrote the following as His testament:[187] **(I).... Paul, a slave of Christ Jesus**, called as an apostle and singled out for God's good news-which He promised long ago through His prophets in the Holy Scriptures-concerning His Son, Jesus Christ our Lord, who was a descendant of David according to the flesh and was established as the powerful Son of God by the resurrection from the dead according to the Spirit of holiness. We have received grace and apostleship through Him to bring about the obedience of faith among all the nations, on behalf of His name, including yourselves who are also Jesus Christ's by calling: To all who are in Rome, loved by God, called as saints. Grace to you and peace from God our Father and the Lord Jesus Christ. First, I thank my God through Jesus Christ for all of you because the news of your faith is being reported in all the

---

[187] Romans 1:1-15

Life Applications of the Holy Spirit

world. For God, whom I serve with my spirit in [telling] the good news about His Son, is my witness that I constantly mention you, always asking in my prayers that if it is somehow in God's will, I may now at last succeed in coming to you."

Because the Apostle Paul is credited with writing the letters which have become most of the New Testament which are read and studied by millions in the Bible today, I think Paul deserves the title to be called the most famous slave in all history who lived some two thousand years. Paul was a slave for Christ, preaching Jesus' core messages of love, mercy, obedience, repentance, and forgiveness, right up until the time he received his freedom from slavery, when he was martyred for the sake of his beliefs in Christ.

...Think about it

.

Brian Smith

You vs. Job

How bad or good do is your life it right now? How does your life measure up to your life's status or your current hope in the future? And what measuring tool is it that you use? Maybe, this is a good time to reflect on the life of Job in the Bible.

The "Book of Job" is the 18th book. It is the oldest book written in the Bible, just not the first in chapters. It is roughly 4,000 years old, and precedes Jesus by a long 2000 years. The Book of Job goes something like this...

Job was a good man. Job loved God, and he feared God. But God allowed one disaster to befall Job after another (while his wife and his friends were never made aware of why). First, Satan stole all his oxen and donkeys, and Satan killed his workers (except one to report the event). Then a fire killed all of his sheep and those watching them except one. Then some raiders stole all is camels and killed his servants except one. Then a tornado hit his brother's home while all his sons and daughters were there and all were killed inside except one. Then Job came down with a disease of boils from head to feet... so much that he became disfigured and hardly recognizable. In his misery and sadness Job wished God would just kill him. But things got worse, his skin filled with worms and his flesh breaks open with pus. Why did these things happen to a good man like Job? Because God thought highly of him in front of Satan, and he told Satan, "Have you considered my SERVANT Job? He is the finest in all the earth- a man of complete integrity. He fears Me, and he will have nothing to do with evil. God had told Satan, test Job; and do with him and his possessions as you wish (but do not harm him), and see if he will curse me to my face." Job never does. Job defends his innocence, and asks why the wicked are not punished. Job speaks of

Life Applications of the Holy Spirit

wisdom and understanding, and Job speaks about his former blessings. Job is challenged by many things which most men will never have to face, while he sits firm in his love for the Lord and then he shows his repentance in his misery. After his test is over, the Lord blesses Job with more than he had in the beginning. In fact, God blesses him with twice as much; with more family and more fortune. Job lived to the age of 140 years, to see four generations of children and grandchildren. It is recorded in the last verse that when he died, he lived a long and good life.[188]

...Think about it.

---

[188] Book of Job

Brian Smith

The Story of Three's

I am going to take us all back to one of our favorite High school chemistry class… so, all you graduated PSJA girls please listen up this time please ok? :-)) If I put a glass of "ice-tap water" on a table with a lid covering the top, how many types of H2O would I have in the glass….1,2, or 3? If you chose 3 this time, you get a "A" for this six-weeks exam and your HS diploma gets reactivated! Ha-ha... So, this a great example of how God, who in His three forms, is all the same. We speak of The Father, The Son, and The Holy Ghost (Spirit). Jesus was the physical form we could have touched in a materialistic world if we had been there two thousand years ago. In John 14:11, Jesus said, "Believe Me, that I am in the Father, and the Father is in Me." Can you see the similarity? This is like saying: you may not understand the fundamentals of biology, chemistry, physics, gravity, electrons, magnetism, cell phones, Wi-Fi___33, sonar, black holes, space travel, core magma, polarity, eggs and mitosis, etc…., etc….etc….but The Father and I are both intrinsically the same. Jesus also said, right before that in John 4:10, "If you knew the Gift of God and who it is that asks you for a drink, you would have asked him and He would have given you living water." When ice melts it transforms into fluid, and it becomes ubiquitous, much like the H2O water which surrounds the H2O ice in the glass. When the H2O ice melts, and goes away, only the H2O water remains; just as when Jesus went to Heaven and He left the Holy Spirit in His place to be all around us (and in us). And there is always some H2O that remains in the glass in all times. It is like God Himself hovering over

Life Applications of the Holy Spirit

the H_2O water, and the H_2O ice, constantly as the invisible H_2O water vapor everywhere. H_2O is even there when the ice and the water are gone in the air along with the nitrogen, oxygen, etc..... H_2O is within us and fills us because we ourselves are made of water as creations (not evolution) of God. In fact, water is the one thing we need 24-7 constantly; even more than food we eat, or we will die and pass this earth, and our bones will return to the ground from which they came. Isn't chemistry class great??? And we think we all are the smart ones who figured this all out.... Well guess what, we did not...From the very beginning God put each of us together perfectly and the world together perfectly also. He showed us His miracles by coming here, and living with us, because He loves each of us in His Trinity-Triune state (Three in One, Father Son and Holy Ghost) and He "God" does not make any trash; in you or in the world! ... And there is nothing any of us can do (as His created beings) to make this world any more perfect than it already is, (because He is in control...For in Him, in His Three worlds, He is in control at all times (not us) no matter how much we all try, think, or believe we are in control. The truth of the matter is, the more we all try to adjust and alter the nature of our Creator to make it better (for our own gain) all we do is temporarily mess things up until He fixes it again.

    ...Think about it.

Brian Smith

Man vs. Mankind

The word "kind" is used many hundreds of times in the Bible…but that is not the whole story.

Let's look at some of the ways that it is referred to because the word "kind" is the root of all things eternal. Some examples are "mankind"[189] "being kind",[190] "kindness",[191] "kindred"[192], "after his kind", [193], "after their kind"[194], "kindly"[195], "kindled"[196], "kinds"[197], "kindleth"[198], "kindreds"[199]

When used by itself "kind" is the single definition of how men should live with others in relationships, whether in marriage, or to strangers, or towards one's self: "Be Kind". Jesus was kind to everyone, and he exemplified the role we should all be taking on this earth of being good stewards in His name. But this does not mean being passive in protecting the blessings or our family of which we are called to do.[200]

---

[189] Genesis 1:26, Leviticus 18:22, 20:13, Job 12:10, I Corinthians 6:9, I Timothy 1:10, James 3:7
[190] Ephesians 4:32
[191] Galatians 5:22
[192] Acts 7:14
[193] Genesis 1:24
[194] Genesis 1:11-12
[195] Genesis 24:19
[196] Genesis 30:2
[197] I Corinthians 14:10
[198] James 3:5
[199] Revelation 1:7, 7: 11:9, 13:7, 14:6
[200] Matthew 21:12-17, Mark 14:16

Life Applications of the Holy Spirit

When used in reference to "of the same kind" the other definitions apply, like "kindred" where things are of the same kind.

Why does the Bible use the word "Mankind" to define us? Because when man was changed over from before Adam and Eve to the image of God, he was given his soul to prepare for eternal life, and made in the same kind as the image of God, and the angels. He was no longer referred to as a man (of evolution), but now a post evolution kind of man which becomes separated from the animals and lowly beast of the world, now created differently from the other's for God's own glory and a new true purpose. Does that make sense?

And for those who choose to do not accept nor prepare for the correct path and direction of the molding required for Eternal life, these end of as kindling to be ashes in fire that does extinguish their creation as a kind of man that is reset, and sends them back to the beginning of the original man (not man-kind) before God chose to intervene and suffer for him on man's behalf.[201]

...Think about it.

---

[201] John 3:16

Brian Smith

Choosing God

When I was a young man... my father gave me some advice to remember regarding love and relationships for when I got older... He very clearly told me, "Don't look for someone who you can just live with, but look for someone you can't live without."[202]

My father and mother were married for 73 years, and their effective lives were a testimony to the commitment which they possessed for each other. And when they passed on to the next world, they each took their separate journey just a week apart from each other. What my father was telling me was that: "with everything that will come to pass in life, marriage will be about commitment, combined with love, to make a long-lasting relationship". Now, as I have grown older with gray hair of my own, I understand his advice also applies to spiritual love combined with spiritual commitment, and is how we choose to have a relationship with our "God". To simplify, what I have realized today is most people are searching for a "God" they can live with; not a "God" they can't live without, much the same way they choose their mate. These are completely two differently ways of life which need to be pointed out. We are all like sheep and goats. We are not all the same, and we are not meant to be. Solid relationships just aren't there with people who want to pick a God they can live with, rather with one they can't live without, and then sooner or later maybe divorce themselves from their "God" if they don't like their choice. That is why... when I refer to my God, I call Him, "My Lord" because He and I have an understanding in our relationship. i.e., I am committed to Him the same, just as much, as in a marriage (and as much a

---

[202] Proverbs 27:17

Life Applications of the Holy Spirit

covenant can be), and He is committed to me.[203] People who refer to "God" as "My God" is this… and "My God" is that… usually will-not refer to "Him as their Lord and Savior" because they have chosen a "God" they have picked out of a line up; one whom they can live with, but not necessarily one they can live without.

They may have opinions (which are great), and if fact they may like to tell them often (even sanctimoniously) but when a person such as I, listen to them it is sort of like listening to investment advice from someone who has no credentials, or child rearing advice from someone who has never had children, or politics from someone who represents a party or a cause, but does not love his people or even him or herself. Do you pick your God… or does He pick you and "Do you answer yes?" Or do you pick your "God" from a line up as one who suits your needs, likes, or dislikes? Do you pick your "God" to be "Your Lord and Savior?" or just something that suits Christmas and Easter needs. Heaven is NOT run like a democracy. For those who don't believe in Jesus as "The Messiah…The Savior of the World", prophecy predicted His birth way before He arrived, and the message signs were stamped all in the skies for a year to prove it. In Matthew 2:16 it says, "When Herod saw that he had been outwitted by the Maji, he was filled with rage. Sending orders, he put to death all the boys in Bethlehem and its vicinity who were two years old and younger, according to the time he had learned from the Maji? So, what was Herod so afraid of? Had Herod perhaps already chosen a "God" he could live with, and now Herod did not want to be a servant to another Lord because he already was "King Herod"?

So, how do you choose your "God" today? Do you not want to give up your position as a king like Herod of you own world? Or will you choose the prophesied one, who walked out of a tomb that could not hold Him, even in death.

…Think about it.

---

[203] Proverbs 16:3

Brian Smith

Creating Second, Third, and Fourth Level Victims

Who will defend the crimes of sinful people before God in the afterlife? Let's take King Herod for instance…In Acts 12, let the record show that: "King Herod arrested some who belonged to the church, with the intention to prosecute them, and he did. He had James, the brother of John, put to death with the sword. When he saw this met approval among the Jews, he proceeded to seize Peter also". In Matthew 2:16, let the record show: "When Herod realized that he had been outwitted by the Magi, and he gave orders to kill all the boys in the vicinity of Bethlehem, and its vicinity who were two years old and under." In Mark 6 let the record show: "When the daughter of Herodias came in and danced, its pleased Herod and his guests. The king said the girl, ask anything you want and I will give it to you. The head of John the Baptist, she answered. The king was distressed, but he immediately sent for an executioner with orders to bring John's head. The man went, beheaded John, and brought his head back on a platter. Herod presented it to the girl, and then she gave it to her mother." But how many second, and third, and forth level victims were created in these families when these deeds were done? The Old Testament says that the sins of the father are carried to the third generation.[204]

King Herod did many terrible things including persecuting Christ's believers, killing innocent children by the thousands, and imprisoning and executing his foes as if they were his personal

---

[204]Deuteronomy 5:9

Life Applications of the Holy Spirit

chattel. I have listened to people today say (2000 years after the resurrection of the Messiah) while they defend some victim whom they do not know (for an injustice committed against them), that they believe that Almighty God is a merciful God, and He will forgive all people REGARDLESS of their actions or REPENTANCE if their HEARTS are SANCTIMONIOUS enough. This is true, [205] but, wow, how the deaf, dumb, and blind can lead others into Hell so easily. This is a terrible thing![206] Beware...Where does everyone believe King Herod's soul is today? True un-believers will not answer for sure, for they know not their own destinies without fore knowledge or concern of fear...

    Eventually, all will all come to the understanding that without Jesus as their Lord[207] and Savior [208], any human action with its best intentions to save themselves or another, will only create another victim somewhere by their own hand... Hate begets hate, and lies beget lies, violence begets violence, war begets war, evil begets evil, and so on... Sooner or later the truth (i.e., Jesus) will win in the end. But, until then, the world can only be the biggest loser in the sum net gain of sin ruled by mortal justice vs. injustice. Only through the power of Jesus Christ's death on the cross, can the world be saved one individual at a time, and not create a secondary victim in the process as the world so chooses to do.

    ...Think about it.

---

[205] I John 1:9, Hebrews 8:12
[206] Matthew 15:14
[207] Philippians 2:9-11
[208] Luke 2:12

Brian Smith

Prodigal Sons[209]

Most everyone has heard of the story of the younger prodigal son who demanded his share of the family estate. He ran off and squandered all his money, then repented, went back to His father who showed complete mercy on him and the father took him back and they celebrated with a feast. But who remembers the "angry older" brother, who was mad because he felt short-changed in his inheritance? The older brother had been "slaving" for his father, was obedient, never disobeying orders, while his younger brother was out living a decadent life. The older brother saw himself as "a victim" because he was supposed to inherit more than he did now. He was the first born; and according to Jewish law, everything was to be given to him… 100%. It was supposed to be his, the first born, who received everything from his birth right of which much was given away.

Jesus was a Jew. His family were all Jews (Hebrews). His biologic Father (Joseph) was a Hebrew, and He most probably was speaking to Jewish people when teaching with this parable, and His twelve students (Disciples) were most likely Jewish; or they all had close Jewish ties.

Peter, was a Jewish Fishermen, who was the first to acknowledge to Jesus the Living Christ, "You are the Messiah, the Son, of the Living God"[210]. This means that Peter, Jesus's Disciple, became the first realized Messianic Jew, who was later designated by Jesus to become the Leader of Jesus's church. Peter later was called

---

[209] Luke 15:11-32
[210] Matthew 16:16

Life Applications of the Holy Spirit

"The Apostle (Missionary) to the Jews"[211], by the Apostle Paul who was called "The Apostle (Missionary) to the Gentiles"[212]. So, what can we take away from these stories?

Jesus was referred to as the Messiah 74 times in the new testament, and He was teaching that any person did not have to be Jewish to inherit the Kingdom of God. The laws of God which had stood for thousands of years had now been modified.

The Jews understood that they were the first born of God, and chosen as God's people through the bloodlines of Abraham,[213] and led by Moses. They had the birth right to the Kingdom of Heaven, but Jesus who's coming had been prophesied as the Messiah, now challenge that birthright. Jesus was teaching now who was going to get into Heaven independent of heritage or bloodlines.

In the prodigal son parable, Jesus taught that there would be a younger brother included, (or group of people) who would share in the estate (the Kingdom of Heaven) if they were repentant, and they would even receive other things that the older brother would not, a fine ring, a fine coat, and fine sandals. The emotion of anger and hostility can easily happen when someone feels like they have been short changed, and also a victim, not of their own doing.

Do you know someone like this, who thinks they were short changed in life even though perhaps they were obedient (or not)? Are they mad at others or the world because they did not get what they think was theirs by birthright? Jesus answered this question of anger in the older son from a Heavenly perspective when Jesus said, "My son,' the father has said, 'you are always with me, and everything I have is yours. But we had to celebrate and be glad, because this brother of yours was dead and is alive again; he was lost and is found.'"[214].

---

[211] Galatians 2:8
[212] Romans 11:13
[213] Deuteronomy 7, Exodus 19:5
[214] Luke 15:31-32

Know that anger is a choice made by men, and is not a heavenly perspective.

…Think about it.

Life Applications of the Holy Spirit

Final Thoughts

If you enjoy reading my posts, then you may also enjoy reading some of my other books. The first book I wrote is called "The Last Three Days of Paul" which was inspired after I watched the "Passion of The Christ". The genre (i.e., category) is Christian Literature: Apologetics. The easiest way to order one my books is to go to the URL: www.DrBrianSmithBooks.com.

Below is some of the book taken from Chapter 12: The Trial of Free Speech. dated May 24th, 68AD, pp 226-227. (Since here is no written historical record of this period in Paul's life, this a heartfelt rendition of what possibly could have happened to Paul during his last hours.)

"When Paul came to the edge of the floor, there was a box in front of him made of cedar wooden planks sitting on the floor. It was about 3 meters by 3 meters by 2 meters, stained with blood and still wet from the last trial. Servius motioned to him to step into the box, because he was about to be spoken to by the Emperor. All three angels came between Paul and the box. They formed an impenetrable barrier that Paul knew was there.

Paul stepped forward one step, stopped, and looked briefly at the box, but he did not step in. The angels then left him for a moment, for it was his hour to shine. He understood the box's meaning: total submission or not. If he stood outside the box, he knew he would be found guilty of being an enemy of Rome, and would not even be given the chance for his case to be addressed. But these were laws of men, not of God. If he were to stand inside the box, then he would be able to speak freely, and testify to the charges against him. Then supposedly a fair judgment would be made accordingly. More often than not, the case was already decided before the accused person had even entered the room, and the box judgment had already been decided.

Paul then stepped over the box and moved toward the center of the rotunda, clearing his throat. Both he and the members knew what this meant: It was a defiance of the rules of order of Rome and of the Emperor himself. Rules were how Rome ran, and rules were to be obeyed. It reminded Paul of what his father had told him so many years ago on that hillside as a young boy looking out over the sea: "Your faith will keep you safe when your friends desert you." Many of the members of the Senate had heard that he could perform miracles, so they were a bit surprised when he moved toward them. Several men in the front row, including the most powerful of the ruling class, stood up and grasped their robes as if ready to run in case he made any quick motion in their direction. Guards who stood at each of the five corridors leading into the chambers proceeded to meet him in the center and surround him with their spears."

Also reflect upon this quote by C.S. Lewis who also wrote Christian literature books in his day on apologetics which included Mere Christianity, "Aim at Heaven and you will get earth thrown in. Aim at earth and you will get neither".

...Think about it.